D0491358

safety in numbers

1 Community Safety and Why It Is Important

Despite some successes in reducing crime, public agencies have not succeeded in tackling the wider issue of community safety.

2 Challenges Facing Community Safety Work

Lessons must be learned from past attempts to promote community safety.

3 Promising Approaches to Promoting Community Safety

Some partnerships have started to achieve breakthroughs in promoting community safety.

4 Conclusion and Way Forward

Both local partnerships and central government need to take short- and medium-term actions.

Contents

© Audit Commission 1999

First published in February 1999 by the Audit Commission for Local Authorities and the National Health Service in England and Wales, 1 Vincent Square, London SW1P 2PN

Printed in the UK for the Audit Commission by Belmont Press

ISBN 1 86240 1314

Photographs: Basildon District Council (p60), Tim Dub/Photofusion (p28), Dyfed-Powys Police Authority (p15), Judy Harrison/Format (p97), Crispin Hughes/Photofusion (57), Debbie Humphry/Photofusion (cover), Sally Lancaster (p45), Craig Mallean/Photofusion (p28), David Mansell (pp5, 6, 11, 24, 67) with thanks to Sunderland City Council and residents of the Pennywell Estate, Hilary Shedel (pp3, 30, 58), Joanne O'Brien/Format (p54), Safer Surrey Partnership (p87), Roderick Smith/Photofusion (p71), David Tothill/Photofusion (p96)

Illustration: David Eaton

Preface

The Audit Commission oversees the external audit of local authorities and National Health Service (NHS) agencies in England and Wales. Additionally, the Commission is required to undertake studies to enable it to make recommendations for improving the economy, efficiency and effectiveness of services provided by these bodies; and it is required to comment on the effects of statutory provisions or guidance by central government on the economy, efficiency and effectiveness of these agencies.

Over the last 15 months the Commission has researched the issue of community safety – one that is topical and impacts directly on all citizens' quality of life. Safety is the key concern for people who live in the country's most deprived areas and, in all areas, there are people for whom fear of crime keeps them housebound and others for whom victimisation has blighted their lives. In economic terms, crime is estimated to cost the UK £50 billion each year.

No single agency has clear responsibility for community safety. As a result, accountability for ensuring that best use is made of public money spent on promoting community safety is unclear. At a time when increasing emphasis is being placed on 'joined-up thinking', it is timely to review how effective public sector interventions have been to date.

This report on community safety follows a series of reports from the Audit Commission that cover the police service, local government and the NHS which increasingly focus on issues of public concern that cut across agencies within the Audit Commission's audit remit [EXHIBIT 1, overleaf]. In particular, this report builds upon the Commission's previous national reports on youth justice (Refs. 1 and 2). These identified the need to move to a more preventative approach, dealing with the causes of offending behaviour as well as its consequences. This report aims to complement and elaborate on that theme, taking the citizen's perspective on the impact of community safety on quality of life.

The Crime and Disorder Act 1998 places a new joint responsibility on local authorities and police forces to work in partnership with relevant agencies and to develop strategies to reduce crime and disorder. If public agencies are to give this new work the priority that it represents for their local communities, then they face a major challenge to their existing ways of working. This report aims to comment on the lessons suggested by past attempts to promote community safety and identify problems and solutions based on current best practice. It also provides a baseline 'snapshot' of progress in developing community safety strategies prior to the implementation of the Crime and Disorder Act.

The report's recommendations will be followed up locally by auditors from April 1999 and more detailed guidance for practitioners will be available on the internet later this year. Future, related studies by the Commission are likely to include a review of economic development and regeneration and tackling drug abuse.

The study on which this report is based was carried out by Laura Hawksworth, Chris Eade and Michael Carpenter of the Local Government Studies Directorate of the Audit Commission, with advice from Judy Renshaw of the Health and Social Services Studies Directorate, under the direction of John Tench and Bob Chilton. Fieldwork for the report took place in ten areas in England and Wales, covering all responsible authorities (principally police and local government) operating in each district or unitary council area. This original research was supplemented by a review of recent literature covering community safety and interviews with experts in the field. Extensive consultation with professional organisations was also conducted, both informally and through representation on the advisory and technical groups (Appendix 3): their co-operation is appreciated. The team was assisted by the expert advice of John Burrows, from MHB Consulting, and also benefited greatly from a national survey of community safety led by Dr Alex Hirschfield of the University of Liverpool, in collaboration with the University of Huddersfield. The conclusions of the report are, however, the responsibility of the Audit Commission alone.

EXHIBIT 1

Related reports by the Audit Commission

This report reflects an increasing emphasis on issues of public concern that cut across departments and agencies within local government and the NHS.

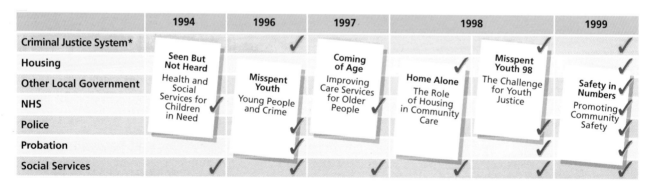

 **Agency covered in report**

* Within the wider criminal justice system, the Audit Commission appoints auditors only to magistrates courts.

Source: Audit Commission

1

Community Safety and Why It Is Important

Despite a focus on crime by some public agencies, wider issues of fear of crime and safety continue to be high on the public agenda. Unsafe communities wreck lives and have a high economic cost. Some public agencies have been forming local partnerships to address community safety, and the new Crime and Disorder Act makes this a statutory duty. A significant challenge lies ahead for new and existing partnerships.

...an unrealistic picture?

Sam lives on a large council estate on the outskirts of a major city. The houses are of good quality, but 15 per cent are unoccupied, some of which have been vandalised and set on fire. One street has been abandoned by all but a lone drug dealer; graffiti and vandalism are part of everyday life. Telephone companies have refused to install public telephones, because they were so often broken into in the past. Transport in and out of the estate is poor.

Sam moved there recently with his mother. They were burgled the night after they moved in. At school he was bullied because his mother was seen 'grassing' to the police. He has made friends, but it can be hard to develop friendships, as many children transfer schools in the middle of the year because their parents leave the estate as soon as they can. Educational attainment at the school is low – as are expectations of getting a job after school. Unemployment on the estate is at 50 per cent.

There is no doctor's surgery on the estate. There is a supermarket and an off-licence at one end, but these look deserted as they always have their shutters down. There used to be a residents' association, but this has not met for five years. When she was burgled, the local police suggested that Sam's mother might try to set up a Neighbourhood Watch scheme, but she felt this was too risky given the way her son has been treated at school.

Sam's mother has asked the housing department if she can be transferred from the estate as soon as possible. The housing officer said that the council was just starting to work with the police to improve safety on the estate...

What is community safety?

1. Community safety is an issue of major public concern. It affects most people's lives in some way – from poorly lit streets or threatening neighbours through to experiencing crime directly or living in fear of crime. It is central to people's quality of life and can make the difference between people wanting to live and work and stay in an area or not. The case described above is based on a site visit made for this report. The kinds of challenges posed by such an unsafe community are at the extreme end of a spectrum of concerns throughout England and Wales.

2. Community safety is an outcome and not a problem or a 'service': it is about people's sense of personal security, which is the product of multiple factors. A precise national definition of community safety does not exist. Commentators have offered a number of broad definitions that suggest that it is concerned with more than crime and aims to prevent, reduce, or at least contain, the things that are most disruptive to people's quality of life [BOX A].

BOX A

Three definitions of community safety

Community safety is concerned with more than crime and aims to get to the heart of what disrupts people's quality of life.

We see community safety as having both social and situational aspects, as being concerned with people, communities and organisations including families, victims and at-risk groups, as well as attempting to reduce particular types of crime and the fear of crime. Community safety should be seen as the legitimate concern of all in the local community.
(Working Group on the Morgan Report)

Community safety is an aspect of quality of life in which people, individually and collectively, are protected as far as possible from hazards or threats that result from the criminal or anti-social behaviour of others, and are equipped or helped to cope with those they do experience. It should enable them to pursue, and obtain fullest benefits from, their social and economic lives without fear or hindrance from crime and disorder.
(Home Office)

Community safety is defined as promoting the concept of community-based action to inhibit and remedy the causes and consequences of criminal, intimidatory and other related anti-social behaviour. Its purpose is to secure sustainable reductions in crime and fear of crime in local communities. Its approach is based on the formulation of multi-agency partnerships between the public, private and voluntary sectors to formulate and introduce community-based measures against crime.
(Local Government Association)

Source: Home Office (Refs. 3 and 4); LGA (Ref. 5)

3. The key to successful community safety approaches is that they address what is directly relevant to people in their local setting; instead of a traditional 'service' approach which provides general reassurance and reacts to problems when they occur, they aim to prevent them from happening in the first place and to reduce their incidence. In order to address the community's fears and concerns properly, community safety work must engage fundamentally with the community in a way that goes beyond the scope of traditional crime prevention work. At the national level, a number of general trends can be detected that build the case for public agencies to focus more on this citizens' point of view.

From responding to crime and victimisation...

4. Crime is an emotive issue for all members of the public, consistently appearing in the top three of the public's list of concerns in surveys (Ref. 6); youth crime featured in the top five election pledges of the Government; and of the Commission's published performance indicators, those related to police performance are viewed as the most important by citizens.

5. Levels of crime are measured by police statistics and the British Crime Survey (BCS).[1] Both measures saw a sharp increase throughout the 1980s, and the drop in police recorded crime since the early 1990s has been reflected in the most recent BCS figures. Overall, BCS crime fell by 14 per cent from 1995 to 1997 [EXHIBIT 2].

---

1   The British Crime Survey asks people about their actual experiences of crime; it indicates that only around half of the crimes that people claim to have experienced are reported to the police, but the level of reporting varies by area and by type of offence. This low level of reporting is in part because people do not think the offence sufficiently serious to report, but is also due to a low expectation of the police's ability to do anything. Not all crimes reported to the police are subsequently recorded: some are found not to be crimes under current definitions; others may be 'duplicates' – that is, reported by more than one person.

EXHIBIT 2

Levels of reported, recorded and British Crime Survey crime in England and Wales

BCS crime fell by 14 per cent from 1995 to 1997.

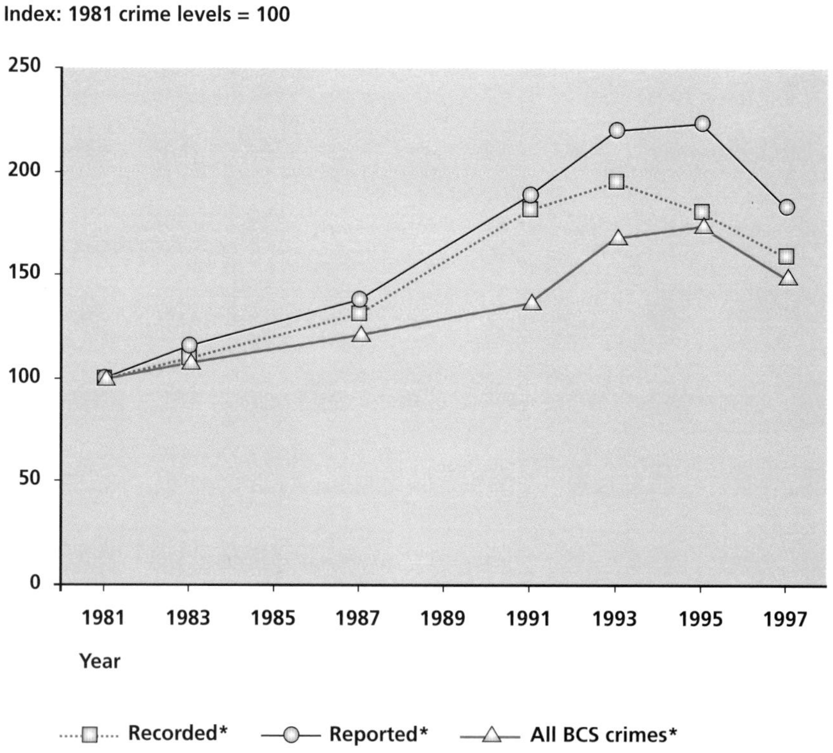

*Note: Recorded and reported crime levels are given for comparable crime categories as the BCS is not comparable with police figures on certain categories, such as common assaults.

Source: British Crime Survey 1998, Home Office (Ref. 7)

Index: 1981 crime levels = 100

Recorded* Reported* All BCS crimes*

Crime affects some communities disproportionately

6. Some specific crimes have had more dramatic reductions than others: for example, while overall BCS crime fell by 14 per cent between 1995 and 1997, household burglary fell by 7 per cent and violent crime fell by 17 per cent over the same period. International comparisons indicate that the UK is relatively safe compared with other countries in respect of violent crime, although the chances of being a victim of robbery, burglary or car crime are higher than in the US (Ref. 8).

7. National averages in recorded crime mask quite extreme variations in incidence between different areas. The hard-hit areas receive much attention from the media. Crime affects some communities disproportionately: over one-half of property crimes and one-third of the victims of those crimes are found in just one-fifth of the population in England and Wales (Ref. 9). People living in areas with the highest crime rates are ten times more likely to be victims of personal crime, and five times as likely to suffer property crime, as those in areas with average levels of crime (Ref. 10). Recorded crime per head of population varies by a factor of three between police force areas [**EXHIBIT 3**].

8. Some individuals suffer repeatedly from crime. The latest BCS shows that 20 per cent of victims of domestic burglary were victimised more than once in a year; of those, 7 per cent were victimised three or more times. Repeat victimisation is a common feature of under-reported crimes, such as racial attacks and domestic violence: often, victims wait until they have been repeatedly attacked before contacting the police. The BCS shows that 55 per cent of victims of domestic violence had been victimised more than once. Research on the 1992 and 1994 BCSs found that between 4 and 5 per cent of respondents consistently suffer 43 per cent of the crimes (Ref. 11).

EXHIBIT 3

Victimisation levels by force in England and Wales, 1997

Recorded crime per head of population varies by a factor of three between police force areas.

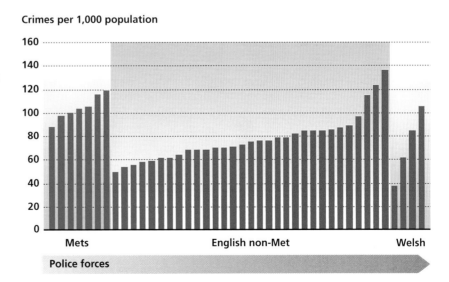

Crimes per 1,000 population

Note: Excludes City of London.

Source: Home Office, Notifiable Offences; Audit Commission, Performance Indicators

9. Victimisation can have serious consequences. Among victims of burglary:

- 40 per cent were 'very upset';
- 20 per cent lost sleep over the incident;
- 23 per cent felt feelings of fear and insecurity for some time after; and
- 33 per cent complained about a sense of invasion of privacy.

The effects of victimisation can also endure: almost one-quarter of victims still report emotional problems six months after the event (Ref. 12). Consequently, the quality of life of affected individuals is intrinsically linked to their sense of safety in the community. Therefore, community safety initiatives by statutory agencies must relate fundamentally to the experiences and anxieties of those who live in insecure neighbourhoods.

...to promoting community safety

10. Fear of crime is more prevalent than crime itself. Most people tend to over-estimate the extent of crime. Only 9 per cent of people were aware that crime had fallen between 1995 and 1997 (Ref. 13). Although only about one-fifth of crime is violent, 58 per cent of people believe that over half of crime is violent. Eight per cent of people indicated that fear of crime had a substantial effect on their quality of life, and 43 per cent said that it had a moderate effect.

11. Fear of crime can affect people's everyday confidence in going out of doors. A recent piece of social research showed that people are becoming more reluctant to open their door to strangers (Ref. 14). Concern about personal safety can discourage many people, especially women, from using public transport. Research reported in the Government's recent transport White Paper indicates that off-peak travel by public transport could grow by 10 per cent if travellers felt safer in making their journeys (Ref. 15). A forthcoming Audit Commission report on transport highlights measures that local authorities could take to improve personal security on public transport.

12. Like crime, the effects of fear of crime are not evenly distributed: they are concentrated within certain communities, and the most vulnerable groups in society are most affected [EXHIBIT 4]. So community safety strategies must deal not only with the wider experiences of the majority of people, but must focus in particular on the needs of communities most at risk. For some, a sense of insecurity in effect places them under a 'curfew'; for others, the concentration of problems in particular neighbourhoods destroys their quality of life.

EXHIBIT 4

Effects of fear of crime on the quality of people's lives

The most vulnerable groups in society are most affected by fear of crime.

*Note: A group of individuals saying that at least four of the following factors – vandalism, rubbish, drugs, teenagers and noisy neighbours – were a big problem in their area.

Source: Home Office, Concern About Crime, 1998 (Ref. 13)

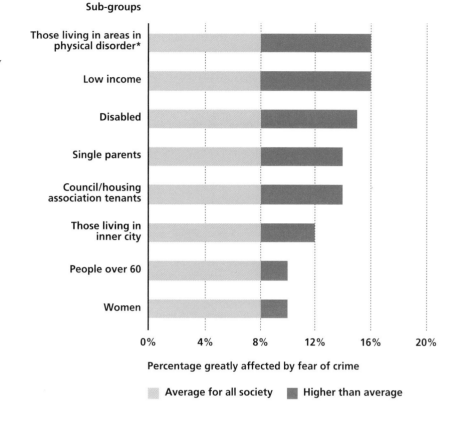

Sub-groups

- Those living in areas in physical disorder*
- Low income
- Disabled
- Single parents
- Council/housing association tenants
- Those living in inner city
- People over 60
- Women

0% 4% 8% 12% 16% 20%

Percentage greatly affected by fear of crime

Average for all society ▮ Higher than average

Community safety strategies in deprived areas need to be comprehensive and tackle the causes of other socially excluding factors

13. The impact of fear of crime on quality of life is most acute in areas of high deprivation. A recent Social Exclusion Unit report (Ref. 16) found that all of the top five dislikes of residents in deprived areas about where they lived concerned safety. Community safety is therefore a central issue within the social exclusion agenda. Community safety strategies in deprived areas need to be comprehensive and tackle the causes of other socially excluding factors, such as unemployment and poor health. It is therefore equally essential that public agencies have an integrated approach to such 'wicked' issues, and many are currently working through the complexities of 'joined-up thinking' [EXHIBIT 5].

14. Although safety is a key concern in deprived neighbourhoods, these are also areas where crimes are least likely to be reported to statutory agencies, so agencies have to work harder to identify, define and solve problems.

15. The BCS found that those living in lower-quality social housing are three times more likely than the average person to be the victim of a personal crime and twice as likely to be the victim of a property crime (Ref. 7). It also found that, over time, there has been a decline in the coverage of household insurance in such areas.

EXHIBIT 5

Community safety in a social exclusion context

It is essential for public agencies to have an integrated approach to issues of social exclusion, and many are currently working through the complexities of 'joined-up thinking'.

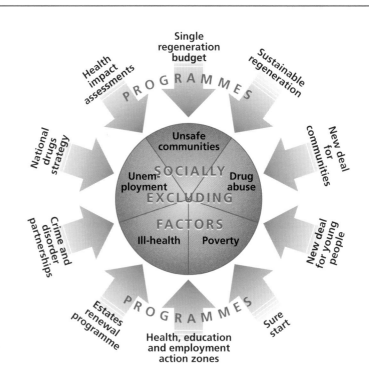

Source: Audit Commission

16. Whether in the most deprived neighbourhoods, or in areas where people simply feel vulnerable, people's fears for their safety are usually affected by a number of factors, only one of which is crime. In many ways, crime is just the 'tip of the iceberg' [EXHIBIT 6].

17. Legal definitions of what constitutes a crime do not capture the full extent of what makes people feel unsafe. No single public agency addresses the more general problem of fear of crime or promotes community safety as an outcome. There is a growing concern in all areas that 'lower-level' problems, such as youth disorder and neighbour nuisance, are not addressed by statutory agencies. One consequence of this is that there is no national information on these 'non-crime' problems, and so their incidence, distribution and trends over time are difficult to quantify.

18. It is often such lower-level disorder that the majority of people suffer and that contributes to high levels of fear of crime. For example, the BCS found that in all areas, but particularly in inner-city areas, various forms of 'disorder' were perceived by residents to be a problem locally [EXHIBIT 7, overleaf].

19. 'Disorder' has no national definition and different police forces record calls to disorder incidents differently. An analysis of disorder calls in one police force area found that a substantial number were classified as 'nuisance', and not formal breaches of the law as such (Ref. 17). Even allowing for problems of interpretation, disorder represents a growing proportion of total police incidents, and calls relating to disorder increased in England and Wales by 19 per cent between 1995/96 and 1997/98 (Ref. 18). Over the same period, the total number of incidents reported to the police actually fell by 6 per cent.

EXHIBIT 6

Community safety

Crime is just the 'tip of the iceberg'.

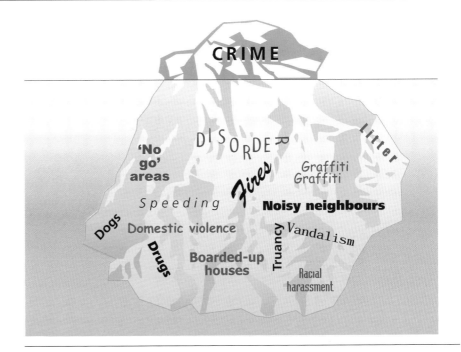

Source: Audit Commission

EXHIBIT 7

Prevalence of disorder

Various forms of 'disorder' were perceived by residents, particularly in inner-city areas, to be a problem.

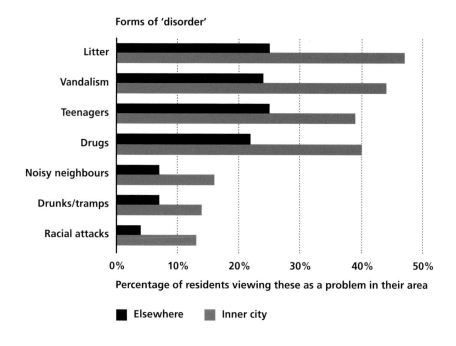

Forms of 'disorder'

Percentage of residents viewing these as a problem in their area

■ Elsewhere ■ Inner city

Source: Home Office, British Crime Survey, 1998

20. Social tension and a disorderly environment also contribute to fear of crime. In 1997, the Institute of Environmental Health Officers recorded its largest increase in complaints about noise and neighbour disputes. Complaints about neighbours have increased by 56 per cent in four years and prosecutions have risen by 98 per cent (Ref. 19). A survey[1] of 14 providers of social housing found that, on average, each had 800 cases of nuisance to deal with in 1996/97. The major complaint was noise (37 per cent) followed by untidy gardens (15 per cent) and criminal behaviour (9 per cent) (Ref. 20). Clearly, safety issues are of concern to housing agencies, although the trend in such problems has not been quantified.

21. There have been attempts to establish a causal link between problems of disorder and crime, although there is no agreement about how such events are linked. Research in the USA has demonstrated that disorder is a reliable predictor of crime and supports the view that *direct action against disorder could have substantial payoffs* in the fight against crime and that disorder *plays an important role in neighbourhood decline* (Refs. 21 and 22). This argument has led to a case being made for initiatives, such as 'zero tolerance' policing, that tackle lower-level problems.

---

[1] Providers of social housing include local authority and voluntary sector housing providers.

Costs of crime

Crime costs are equivalent to 5 per cent of GNP in many developed countries

22. Not everyone has to live in unsafe areas but, because the consequences are funded through taxation and insurance, the problem is shared across society and so, in effect, everyone pays. Data is not available on the wider costs of fear of crime and disorder, but in 1993 the Home Office estimated that crime was costing the UK economy £31 billion annually and by 1998 had increased its estimate to £50 billion (Ref. 23). The International Centre for Crime Prevention estimates that crime costs are equivalent to 5 per cent of GNP in many developed countries (Ref. 24).

23. Where insurance is available premiums will, to some extent, even out the cost, although insurers are increasingly 'cherry picking' to compete for customers. The total value of household claims to replace losses due to burglary currently runs at £513 million per year in the UK (Ref. 25). Private businesses suffer too: the retail crime bill is estimated to be £1.42 billion (Ref. 26). Both rural and metropolitan areas are affected. The UK private security industry has quadrupled in size since 1971 and now employs 300,000 guards, more than twice the number of police officers (Ref. 27).

24. Community safety is no less of a problem for public services. A few agencies have been able to quantify the costs in their area. Examples include:

- a study of the costs of vandalism in schools in Scotland estimated that the bill for insuring against vandalism and damage was higher than the amount spent on books each year (Ref. 28);

- Salford Housing Department estimated that anti-social behaviour by tenants cost it £2 million per year;

- a study of responses to domestic violence in the London Borough of Hackney estimated that the problem cost £5 million in 1996/97 per year, borne by public agencies across the borough (Ref. 29); and

- a study of the costs of crime in Hull estimated that overall the cost to the City was £177 million per annum, comprising £37 million in crime prevention measures, £49 million responding to crime and £30 million in prosecuting and dealing with offenders (Ref. 30).

25. Nor is the cost confined to local government and the police. An NHS trust in Merthyr Tydfil estimated that the costs of securing the hospital were in the region of £100,000 per year. The NHS Executive has recognised the issue nationally and is issuing advice to deal with staff assaults and stress; it has also issued guidelines on how to estimate the cost of crime to NHS trusts (Ref. 31). A recent review by the Royal College of Nursing and the NHS Executive has produced guidance for staff on how to manage the problem of violent incidents that NHS staff working in the community may have to deal with (Ref. 32).

26. Therefore, not only is there an imperative from the point of view of the citizen – both individually and communally – to address community safety, but there are also strong managerial and economic arguments for giving attention to this growing problem.

Role of public agencies

27. Public agencies have responded to this call to increase the citizen focus and to broaden the agenda from crime to community safety. A number of developments have been taking place over recent years at both the national and local levels.

National role

28. In the past, central government has managed issues of community safety largely through providing direction and guidance to local agencies, such as the police. Local government involvement was first actively promoted by government through a joint departmental circular issued in 1984 (Ref. 33). The most significant development was perhaps the Morgan Report (Ref. 3), which recommended that there should be *a clear statutory responsibility [on local authorities] for the development and stimulation of community safety activities*, with funding from central government for this new duty. Both of these core proposals were rejected by the government of the day. The Crime and Disorder Act 1998 marks a change of emphasis (Ref. 34).

29. A key role for central government is the allocation of resources to different parts of the public sector. It is just as difficult to quantify the resources devoted to preventing crime at the national level as it is for local agencies. Commentators have pointed out that the £9 billion spent on the criminal justice system in England and Wales has dwarfed resources specifically earmarked for crime prevention (Ref. 35).

30. Under the last Government, a number of 'challenge funds' were set up to enable local agencies to bid for central resources to meet local needs. All of these initiatives have catalysed early local work on community safety [TABLE 1].

TABLE 1

Major recent central government funding available for local work on community safety in England

Fund	Lead department	Funding and duration
Safer Cities Phase I (1988-93)	Home Office	£22m over 7 yrs
Safer Cities Phase II (1993-97)	DETR/Home Office	£16m over 4 yrs
CCTV challenge fund (1995-98)	Home Office	£38.5m over 4 yrs
Single Regeneration Budget (1993-)	DETR	£3.46bn over last 4 years (£2bn over next 3 years)

Source: Home Office; DETR

31. In Wales, the responsibility and funding for all new Strategic Development Scheme (SDS) approvals has been delegated to local authorities. The SDS supports a very wide range of economic, environmental and social projects and separate figures on community safety are not available. The future availability and level of SDS funding from 1999-2000 onwards has yet to be finalised.

32. The Safer Cities Phase I funding went to 20 sites in England and Wales and typically sponsored 180 local projects per site. A partnership approach was required, and these partnerships often added locally to resources through local fundraising and agency contributions, bringing total project funding to £40 million. Phase II funding covered 29 sites in England and Wales. Of these, an average 51 crime prevention/community safety schemes were funded at each site, and the Safer Cities grant typically accounted for around half the total cost of each scheme.

33. The Single Regeneration Budget (SRB in England) has funded local regeneration schemes that have increasingly included a community safety component [BOX B, overleaf]. The Government Offices of the Regions now administer these schemes, but grants are awarded to whole programmes of work and amounts spent on community safety are not recorded separately. This work is set to continue under the current government.

Local regeneration schemes have increasingly included a community safety component

BOX B

Single Regeneration Budget and community safety in England

The SRB is a fund administered by the DETR to support regeneration initiatives in England that have increasingly included a community safety component and are carried out by local partnerships. It addresses a wide number of issues: employment; education and skills; social exclusion; sustainable regeneration; local economies; and 'tackling crime and drug abuse and improving community safety'. The scheme is currently in its fifth round and has so far allocated over £3.46 billion to a wide range of schemes and initiatives across England. In a sense, all of this funding could be said to address community safety issues, either directly, or indirectly, by addressing the underlying causes of community insecurity. In fact, an analysis of successful bids shows the rising profile of community safety within SRB.

Percentage of SRB projects with community safety-related outcomes

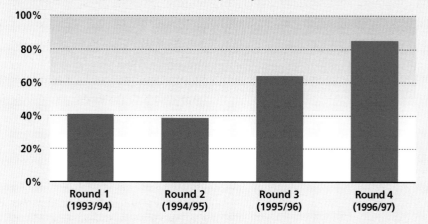

Source: Audit Commission survey of DETR reports

For the 1995/96 and 1996/97 rounds to date (for which £2.26 million has been allocated) it is estimated that, to date, the following outcomes have been achieved:

- one million people have benefited from community safety initiatives;

- 17,000 buildings have had their security upgraded;

- 1,000 community safety initiatives have been created; and

- 24,000 youths have attended over 600 youth crime prevention initiatives.

The future

The Government hopes to continue the SRB scheme to at least 2002, although future rounds will be administered regionally.

Source: Audit Commission analysis of DETR reports

Different central government departments are responsible for different aspects of the community safety agenda

34. Different central government departments are responsible for different aspects of the community safety agenda. Within Whitehall, the Home Office has tended to take the lead on crime prevention; it has a strong reputation for furthering research into 'what works'. The Crime Prevention Agency was set up in 1996 to promote a preventative approach to crime problems. The Home Office also oversees adult and youth justice issues through the probation service. In addition to Safer Cities, the Home Office has sponsored a number of local CCTV schemes, through a challenge fund that came to an end in 1998. This sponsorship has been influential in steering many local partnerships towards investment in CCTV schemes. The DETR has led on regeneration and the second phase of the Safer Cities Scheme. The Department of Health is involved in youth justice through its social services work and the NHS Executive has increasingly developed a role in advising NHS trusts on security and staff safety.

35. In Wales, the Welsh Office has responsibility for areas that in England are covered by a number of Whitehall departments, allowing for a more holistic approach. Responsibility for crime and disorder and the police rests with the Home Office, however, and the Secretary of State for Wales has no statutory role in these areas. For example, the Home Office has retained oversight of the three Phase II Safer Cities projects. This fragmented picture at the national level has not helped local agencies to co-ordinate approaches across their own departments and between agencies.

Local role

36. The police service has always had a crime prevention role – the principal remit of the Metropolitan Police was defined in 1829 by its first Commissioners, Rowan and Mayne, as the prevention of crime. It is difficult to quantify the resources that the police currently devote to this activity, but few officers work full-time on crime prevention – about 1 per cent of force strength, on average (Ref. 36). A recent inspection report called for 'unequivocal leadership' to reduce crime and added that 'A strong feeling amongst police practitioners is that the Home Secretary's key objectives for policing in 1997/98 and previous years, have encouraged (crime) detection not reduction' (Ref. 37). The police service has also been instrumental in supporting a growing number of Neighbourhood Watch schemes. Finally, the statutory consultation mechanisms on the annual policing plan, set up initially by the Police and Criminal Evidence Act, 1984, have also brought the police more closely in touch with local communities' broader safety concerns.

Many public agencies have recognised the value of working in partnership to make more of scarce resources

37. Local government involvement in community safety activities dates back to the early 1980s, by which point some local authorities had already developed community safety strategies. Despite central government's rejection of several key recommendations in the Morgan Report (Ref. 3), local authority involvement and enthusiasm continued to grow. One reason has been, quite simply, public demand. Local government has found, through a variety of channels – from individual representations to councillors through to formal surveys – that crime represents a growing concern among local people. One fieldwork district council surveyed its local communities in 1992, asking what key functions they wished the council to perform. At the last minute, crime prevention was added to the choices presented. It came top of the list, and the council began working on community safety from that point. Another reason has undoubtedly been the availability of central government Challenge Fund money, together with grants for partnership and other approaches to promoting safer communities.

38. Consequently, it is not surprising that a survey of local authorities in June 1996 found that many had already started to do work in this field (Ref. 38). The main findings were that:

- 53 per cent of respondent authorities had published a policy statement on community safety;

- 51 per cent had a separately identified budget for community safety;

- 37 per cent had community safety co-ordinators (although almost one-third of these were part-time); and

- 35 per cent had conducted a crime audit to monitor the success of local initiatives.

Since that 1996 survey the picture has been updated, showing that one-half of local authorities and three-quarters of police forces claimed to have strategies in place by March 1998 (Ref. 39).

39. Many public agencies have recognised the value of working in partnership to make more of scarce resources to solve these complex problems. However, such attempts have not taken place within a national framework, but have tended to rely on the skill and motivation of local communities, agencies and sometimes departments within those agencies. Ownership of the problem of unsafe communities has therefore been patchy and unclear.

Significant change required

40. The national picture is changing rapidly. Most significantly, the Government has responded to the issue of 'who owns the community safety problem' by introducing new duties for crime and disorder prevention in the Crime and Disorder Act. Crime and disorder are core problems in unsafe communities. The Act aims to put community safety issues firmly on the map by placing a duty on local councils and police forces as 'responsible authorities' to lead on crime and disorder prevention, in partnership with police authorities, probation committees, health authorities, fire brigades and other agencies [EXHIBIT 8].

EXHIBIT 8

Provisions for partnership working in the Crime and Disorder Act

The Act aims to put community safety issues firmly on the map by placing a duty on local government and the police as 'responsible authorities' to lead on crime and disorder in partnership with other agencies.

Crime and Disorder Act Statutory Framework

Local authorities and police forces are required to:

- *form statutory partnerships* with other prescribed authorities (health authorities, probation, magistrates courts, CPS and the voluntary sector) at the level of the district or unitary council. The Act requires the chief constable and the chief executives of the local authorities to form the partnership as joint leaders. In addition to those prescribed authorities, they can invite others – such as existing partnerships and voluntary agencies – on to the partnership at their discretion;

- *conduct an audit* of crime and disorder across the local authority area, using the relevant data from partner agencies;

- *consult the public* at key stages in strategy development, notably on the results of the audit and on identifying the targets for agencies to aim for;

- *draw up three-year community safety strategies* with short and long-term targets for reducing crime and disorder; and

- *monitor and evaluate* this work systematically; all initiatives are to be *monitored*, but with selective evaluation so as to learn from new types of initiatives without reinventing the wheel.

Source: Crime and Disorder Act, 1998, (Ref. 34) (see Appendix 1)

41. Furthermore, the new Government has attempted, through its comprehensive spending review, to reallocate spending to crime prevention. Clearly this is a long-term change, and the review identified £250 million over three years for the national crime reduction strategy (Ref. 40). Key elements of the strategy include:

- a national focus on a number of examples of successful crime reduction strategies;

- use of some of the £250 million as seedcorn money to encourage investment in finding out 'what works'; and

- the development of 12 'pathfinder projects' around England and Wales from which to learn national lessons.

Health, Employment and Education Action Zones address many of the underlying risk factors associated with community safety

42. The Crime Prevention Agency is currently developing a database on 'what works' and – through the Crime Prevention College – is co-ordinating national training agencies and other providers of training to focus on the development of the most urgently needed skills in this new field. The Home Office – together with other agencies – is developing a number of performance indicators, focusing in particular on the national performance framework for policing, to underpin the emphasis on promoting safety.

43. The new Welsh Office initiative to tackle social exclusion – the 'People in Communities' programme – will provide a focus for co-ordinated action in deprived communities in Wales. Eight communities have been identified as 'beacons', or flagships. These beacons are tasked with exploring the ways in which community-led analysis of problems and proposals to deal with them can deliver sustainable improvements to the social, economic and environmental circumstances of these communities. Crime prevention and community safety are likely to be key elements in the strategies which these communities devise.

44. In addressing the need for a co-ordinated approach, the recent Social Exclusion Unit paper concentrated on communities where work to enhance safety is most needed; it identified a role for 18 cross-cutting teams within government to co-ordinate issues that cross departmental boundaries (Ref. 16). The Crime Prevention Agency is moving into this role of broker between departments to encourage a cross-government approach to community safety.

45. Competitive bids are still a feature of the Government's approach – a number of recently announced community safety initiatives can have impact, either directly or indirectly, by tackling underlying problems:

- New Deal for Communities (£800 million over three years);
- Single Regeneration Budget (£2 billion over the next three years for existing and new schemes); and
- Sure Start – early education (£540 million over three years).

46. In addition to new funding, other national initiatives form part of the context for current community safety work. Health, Employment and Education Action Zones address many of the underlying risk factors associated with community safety, and the awarding of 'zone' status to areas will mean that local agencies need to integrate this activity with that of local community safety partnerships. Similar initiatives are being developed in Wales.

47. Finally, the accountability and performance regimes for both local government and the police service are changing. The forthcoming duty of best value will require authorities to demonstrate improvements in services, by:

- *challenging* the rationale for key activities or means of delivering services;
- *consulting* local people on these objectives;
- *comparing* performance with other authorities, other agencies and the private sector; and
- *competing* with alternative providers in the market place to demonstrate that their services represent good value.

The provisions for partnership working in the Crime and Disorder Act reflect much of this emphasis on accountability and performance, particularly on challenging the objectives of locally developed strategies and consulting local communities.

48. All this adds up to a substantial change agenda for local agencies. As authorities are now starting to draw up their first strategies, it is time to take stock of what has gone before and to learn the lessons of what has worked well and what has not. A narrow approach to complying with the Crime and Disorder Act is unlikely to make a sustainable impact on the quality of life of people living in unsafe communities, and this report aims to describe the problems of the past, tease out the lessons and comment on current and best practice.

Conclusion

49. No single agency has clear responsibility or authority to address crime and fear of crime. Yet these are often top of any list of concerns that citizens wish to see addressed. Given the uncertain legal framework, many agencies – public and private – have struggled to address these complex issues and concerns. This report examines current and past initiatives in the context of existing and proposed legislation, identifies best practice and suggests a way forward.

50. This chapter has attempted to outline the context. Chapter 2 goes on to identify key problems with past community safety work, drawing on in-depth fieldwork in ten sites around the country as well as national and local research findings where relevant. Chapter 3 proposes solutions to these problems for local agencies, commenting on good practice and making recommendations for change. It also identifies the emerging national role that is needed to support local agencies. Chapter 4 provides a brief conclusion, discusses the way forward and summarises the recommendations for each group of stakeholders.

2

Challenges Facing Community Safety Work

Many local agencies have already attempted to tackle
community safety. Past attempts have often been one-off
projects that have not been owned by partner
organisations. They have often not reflected local people's
priorities and have failed to invest sufficiently in effective
preventative strategies.

Despite a large number of initiatives, the problem of community insecurity persists

51. New legislation provides the backdrop to this report. The Crime and Disorder Act advocates a partnership approach to the complex problems of unsafe communities, but past experience highlights a number of problems with partnership working which the new statutory partnerships will need to overcome. Despite a large number of initiatives, the problem of community insecurity persists, signalling a need to review the efficacy of these early initiatives.

52. There is much experience in both England and Wales from which to learn. A survey of local authorities indicated that, in 1996, over half of local authorities had produced some form of policy document covering community safety (Ref. 38). Of the ten sites visited for this study, seven had community safety strategies. But drafting a strategy is not an end in itself. Such strategies are valuable only if they launch co-ordinated and relevant initiatives which work. Identifying 'what works', where, in what circumstances, and why, is therefore crucial to working successfully on community safety.

53. This chapter discusses the main problems confronting those local agencies that have tried to put community safety strategies into practice. The problems span the process of developing strategies through to delivering outcomes and reflect some of the general difficulties in reconciling a bottom-up, preventative approach with a more traditional, service-led approach with national objectives. Many current strategies:

- do not reflect local people's priorities;
- are weak on the causes of crime;
- fail to invest sufficiently in prevention;
- are unclear on the rationale for working in partnership; and
- lack integration with mainstream activities [**EXHIBIT 9**].

EXHIBIT 9

The main problems confronting local agencies

This chapter discusses the five main problems confronting those local agencies that have tried to put community safety strategies into practice.

Many current stategies...

...do not reflect local people's priorities

...fail to invest sufficiently in prevention

...lack integration with mainstream activities

...are weak on the causes of crime

...are unclear on the rationale for working in partnership

Source: Audit Commission

Not reflecting local people's priorities

Consulting local people has not typically formed part of the process of identifying community safety problems

54. Since community safety aims to address local people's concerns about safety in their area, a natural way to start developing a strategy is to ask people to identify the problems. Besides knowing about local problems, people may well be able to contribute ideas on how to solve them. Agencies may or may not have the full picture from their management information, not least because of non-reporting by victims: for example, the BCS contains unpublished evidence that in heavily victimised areas, the proportion of offences reported to the police falls (Ref. 41). Moreover, consultation can generate ownership of problems and thereby harness the attention and resources of local people.

55. Despite the importance of local people's views, the degree to which agencies in fieldwork sites had either understood or accommodated local people's concerns was variable. This was due to:

- insufficient emphasis being given to obtaining the views of local residents;

- information about community concerns not being brought together in a systematic way; and

- a tension between bottom-up strategies that prioritised local people's concerns and the priorities set either nationally or corporately across partner agencies.

Insufficient emphasis on obtaining the views of local communities

56. To date, consulting local people has not typically formed part of the process of identifying community safety problems. A national sample in March 1998 found that only 57 per cent of police forces and 44 per cent of local authorities had used public consultation to inform audits of local community safety problems (Ref. 39).

57. Even where consultation has taken place, it has not always focused on those in greatest need. For example, experience with Safer Cities projects revealed that *rather than identifying and developing the potential of key individuals and groups to run particular schemes, co-ordinators simply responded to the scheme proposals that were submitted* (Ref. 42). Consequently, crime prevention projects were less likely to exist in those higher crime areas where they were most needed, since residents in such areas were less confident in coming forward. Added to this, externally funded projects often suffered from tight deadlines for submitting bids, often at the cost of consulting fully with local people.

58. Consulting local people about their concerns is a difficult process – agencies often underestimated the nature of the challenge. Simply asking members of the public to list general concerns often left staff with an unclear understanding of the extent or causes of a problem. For example, at one site a concern expressed about youth disorder during consultation did not provide the partnership with enough information to take action. Questions went unanswered about when and why these problems arose, and with what frequency.

59. Having gained a general picture of problems across an authority, partnerships need to focus on areas of concern. Particular problems exist with 'hard-to-reach' groups, such as ethnic minority communities and victims of domestic violence, whose experiences may not feature in general surveys or public forums. Victims may be too frightened to come forward or may feel alienated by the current approaches of statutory agencies. Data within agencies on such 'hidden problems' is likely to be poor: estimates are that just 34 per cent of violence incidents where the perpetrator is known to the victim and 26 per cent of domestic violence incidents are reported to the police (Ref. 7). Staff in agencies sometimes find local groups hard to work with once dialogue is established [**BOX C**].

60. Consultation, if done properly, can be expensive. Public surveys alone typically cost in the region of £6,000-£20,000, and these often need to be supplemented by focus groups and regular forums. Community development exercises require a longer-term investment – one site spent £472,000 over five years.

61. In summary, the experience of consultation on community safety is that it has often been given insufficient emphasis and has generated a general list of issues rather than helped authorities to target their work.

BOX C

Challenges in consulting hard-to-reach groups

In one London borough, attempts were made to consult representatives of ethnic minority groups on issues of racial harassment. Staff found two active groups, which were particularly valuable since they had knowledge about victims and incidents and the consequences of racial harassment.

However, these groups did not agree with aspects of the council's strategy. They were annoyed that local authority and tenants' and residents' associations were trying to shift the focus of the council's work away from racial harassment to harassment in general. They began attending key council meetings, publicised their concerns through the local media and mounted legal challenges to council practices. These tactics were successful in drawing public attention to problems of racial harassment.

Eventually it was made a requirement of Safer Cities funding that the groups were involved as partners, despite protests from local authority staff and tenants' groups.

Source: Police Research Group Paper 67 (Ref. 43)

Unplanned approach to consultation

62. Consultation with local people can take many different forms. Partner agencies have used a number of mechanisms to discover the concerns of local people, with the most common being public meetings [**EXHIBIT 10**].

63. While public meetings can offer opportunities for dialogue and be valuable in gauging general views, they tend to reflect the views of those who turn up. Staff frequently expressed the concern that these views were rarely representative, and an over-reliance on this one mechanism is unlikely to give a balanced picture. Such meetings have their place, but do not enable partnerships to quantify people's views and prioritise or track changes over time.

EXHIBIT 10

Forms of public consultation on community safety

The most common form of consultation was public meetings.

Focus groups 20%

Public meetings 65%

Other 5%

Surveys 10%

Source: Universities of Liverpool and Huddersfield Survey (Ref. 39)

Information from services that might inform community safety strategies rarely reached those drawing up such strategies

64. In general, consultation exercises were not well co-ordinated and tended to ask the same groups about similar issues on different occasions, potentially causing 'survey fatigue'. As well as consultation by the partnership, other individual agencies conducted their own consultation exercises, frequently identifying community safety issues as a by-product. For example, housing tenancy forums, police community consultative groups, and social services family forums often raised concerns about safety. However, information from these services that might inform community safety strategies rarely reached those drawing up such strategies, since there were usually no mechanisms for collating it. In fact, only two out of the ten sites had a communications strategy for community safety.

Tension between top-down and bottom-up approaches

65. Where consultation had taken place, local people typically expressed greater concern about disorder and lower-level crimes than about serious crimes. Consultation rarely invited them to make trade offs between these competing concerns. Within fieldwork sites, a number of common themes emerged [**EXHIBIT 11**].

EXHIBIT 11

Current public safety concerns

Common concerns about community safety do not always focus on serious crimes.

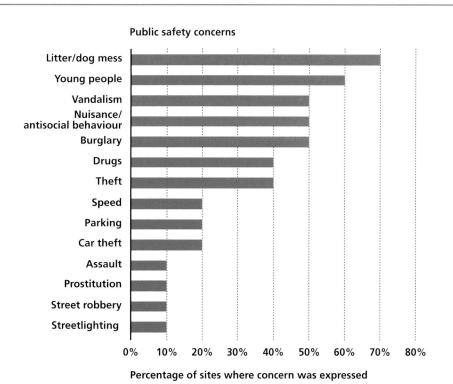

Public safety concerns

Percentage of sites where concern was expressed

Source: Audit Commission fieldwork

66. Staff in fieldwork sites identified tensions between an approach to strategy development that starts from local people's views and one that starts from nationally or corporately set objectives. For example, this tension was seen starkly by police managers, who needed to balance the Home Secretary's national objectives in the statutory policing plan, which emphasise more serious crime, with local demands for more tailored approaches [EXHIBIT 12].

67. The national priority to target more serious offences is likely to result in a lower priority being accorded to lower-level local problems. As a result, when asked what they would prioritise, those drawing up strategies within statutory agencies generally gave a lower priority to some of the non-criminal issues that most commonly concern local people [EXHIBIT 13]. Similarly, careful geographic targeting within a county council area could result in resources being withdrawn from some district councils with fewer serious crime problems.

68. The requirements to fulfil national, top-down requirements may thus inadvertently weaken the link between community safety work and the concerns of local communities.

EXHIBIT 12

National, corporate and local priorities for the police

Police managers need to balance acievement of the Home Secretary's national objectives with local demands for more tailored approaches.

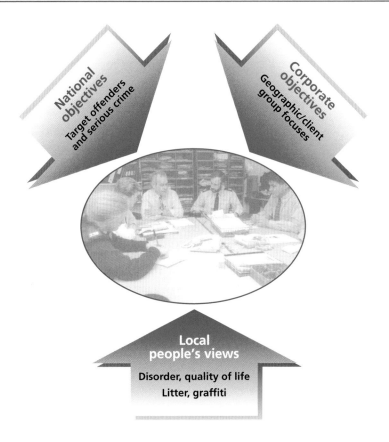

Source: Audit Commission

EXHIBIT 13

Highest and lowest priorities for statutory agencies

Staff within statutory agencies generally gave a lower priority to the concerns most commonly expressed by local people.

POLICE FORCES

Top 5 priorities

1.... **Repeat domestic burglary**
2.... **Fear of crime**
3.... **Domestic burglary**
4.... **Child abuse**
5.... **Drugs-related offences**

Lowest 5 priorities

5.... **Minor disorder**
4.... **Vandalism/graffiti**
3.... **Safety on public transport**
2.... **Parks/open spaces**
1.... **Neighbour disputes**

LOCAL AUTHORITIES

Top 5 priorities

1.... **Fear of crime**
2.... **Housing estates**
3.... **Juvenile disturbances**
4.... **Drugs-related offences**
5.... **Alcohol-related offences**

Lowest 5 priorities

5.... **Business/commercial crime**
4.... **Robbery**
3.... **Hate crime**
2.... **Safety on public transport**
1.... **Minor disorder**

Source: Universities of Liverpool and Huddersfield survey (Ref. 39).

Weak on the causes of crime

69. Any attempt to tackle the problem of unsafe communities requires an analysis of the causes of such problems and some notion of what might work in addressing them, and why. It is not possible to identify single solutions that work in most settings. What works on a sustained basis in a particular community will often be specific and tailored to its circumstances. Therefore, there are no 'off-the-shelf' national solutions to community safety. What are needed are intelligent processes that identify problems and define remedies and methods of local evaluation.

70. The starting point for developing a strategy should be to prioritise problems across an area and analyse their causes. Only then can a sensible effort be made to tackle these problems, and learn from existing efforts about what works. This structured approach to strategy development has been pioneered within the police service, under the term 'problem-oriented policing' or, more generally, as the 'problem-solving approach'. Problem-solving techniques were not evident in fieldwork sites due to:

• limited mapping and analysis of problems;

• a lack of understanding of 'what works'; and

• insufficient monitoring and evaluation.

Analysis of problems

71. Nevertheless, there is a growing consensus internationally on the factors that contribute to unsafe communities and which increase the likelihood of crime and offending behaviour. Known as 'risk factors', such indicators are not causes of crime as such, but the likelihood of criminality increases with their intensity or clustering [EXHIBIT 14]. Mapping such risk factors provides a good information base for examining the risk of community insecurity in a particular area.

EXHIBIT 14

Risk factors for unsafe communities

Risk factors are not causes of crime as such, but the likelihood of criminality increases as their intensity or clustering increases.

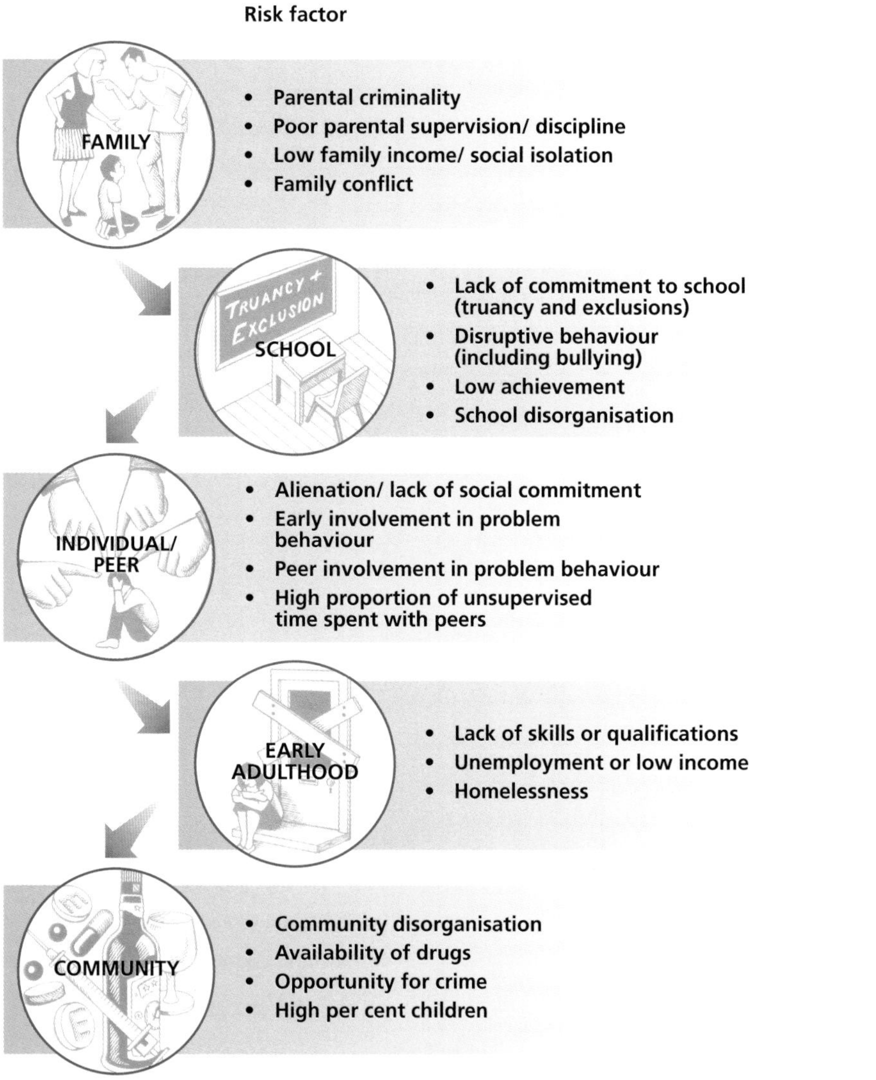

Risk factor

FAMILY
- Parental criminality
- Poor parental supervision/ discipline
- Low family income/ social isolation
- Family conflict

SCHOOL (TRUANCY + EXCLUSION)
- Lack of commitment to school (truancy and exclusions)
- Disruptive behaviour (including bullying)
- Low achievement
- School disorganisation

INDIVIDUAL/ PEER
- Alienation/ lack of social commitment
- Early involvement in problem behaviour
- Peer involvement in problem behaviour
- High proportion of unsupervised time spent with peers

EARLY ADULTHOOD
- Lack of skills or qualifications
- Unemployment or low income
- Homelessness

COMMUNITY
- Community disorganisation
- Availability of drugs
- Opportunity for crime
- High per cent children

Source: Turning the Tide, (Ref. 35)

Past audits have tended to depend heavily on police data, which is likely to be narrowly focused on reported crime

72. The Crime and Disorder Act requires partnerships to conduct an audit of problems within their area; this requirement had been anticipated in many of the fieldwork sites [**EXHIBIT 15**].

73. This work is a useful start, but the approaches to date have focused on neighbourhoods within a council area; few partnerships used audits to establish priorities *across* unitary or district council areas, or to provide the baselines required for monitoring across the area and thereby learn locally about what works. In their current form, therefore, such audits are not the strategic exercise envisaged by the Act.

74. Past audits have tended to depend heavily on police data, which is likely to be narrowly focused on reported crime. While police data was often readily available in analysable form, the BCS demonstrates that just 44 per cent of crimes are reported to the police, so using this data alone would at the very least understate problems, if not provide a distorted picture. The involvement of staff from each agency, using relevant data from each agency, is more likely to commit all partners to the conclusions of the audit. Finally, an over-dependence on data about actual incidents meant that many of the audits did not address risk factors, since data on people's lifestyles – if collected at all – would more likely be present in other agencies' data sets.

EXHIBIT 15

Neighbourhood audits conducted in advance of the Crime and Disorder Act

Many of the fieldwork sites had already conducted some form of audit of community safety problems in their area.

Problem	A	B	C	D	E	F	G	H	I	J
Audit conducted?	✗	✓	✓	✓	✓	✓	✓	✓	✓	✓
Authority-wide?	✗	✗	✓	✗	✓	✗	✗	✗	✗	✓
Specific neighbourhood?	✗	✓	✓	✓	✓	✓	✓	✓	✓	✓
Data										
Beyond police data to multi-agency?	✗	✗	✓	✓	✓	✓	✓	✗	✗	✓
Risk factors?	✗	✗	✓	✓	✓	✓	✓	✗	✗	✓
Community views?	✗	✗	✓	✗	✓	✓	✓	✗	✓	✓
Analysis										
'Hot spots'?	✗	✗	✓	✓	✓	✓	✓	✗	✗	✓
Trends?	✗	✓	✓	✓	✓	✗	✗	✗	✗	✗
Existing activities										
Have they been reviewed?	✗	✗	✓	✗	✗	✗	✗	✗	✗	✓
In-house/external										
Used in-house expertise?	✗	✓	✗	✗	✗	✗	✗	✓	✓	✗

Source: Audit Commission fieldwork

Most audits failed to analyse data in a way that enabled them to focus action

75. Most audits failed to analyse data in a way that enabled them to focus action. The better audits were able to identify 'hot spots' or concentrations of problems. For example, in one local authority, 40 per cent of domestic burglaries occurred in a neighbourhood where only 10 per cent of the population lived. Similarly, in many cases, the lack of a trend of data made it difficult to ascertain whether the problems were enduring, or were merely 'blips' that might disappear by themselves if no intervention took place.

76. Having audited problems within an area, it would seem sensible to map existing activities that may already be addressing those problems. This work was not always evident, leaving open the possibility that any new initiatives would inadvertently duplicate existing efforts.

77. Finally, many audits had been conducted by external consultants. This was especially common where sites had been involved in Safer Cities and SRB schemes. Organisations such as NACRO and Crime Concern had contributed useful expertise, but this expertise was often not transferred to the commissioning authority. Consequently, work started by consultants was rarely updated.

Poor understanding of 'what works'

78. In attempting to develop options for addressing local problems, there is – once again – a growing, but not complete, body of research into 'what works' to promote community safety. The most authoritative recent study was commissioned by the US Department of Justice and conducted by Larry Sherman (Ref. 44). This evaluated 500 initiatives and classified crime prevention practices into: 'what works' – programmes that prevent crime or reduce risk factors in the kinds of contexts in which they have been evaluated, and should therefore also work in similar contexts; 'what's promising' – programmes that need further research to judge whether they could work elsewhere, but which have shown promising results; and programmes that have shown no evidence of working.

79. The level of evaluative sophistication used by Sherman cannot realistically be expected within local community safety strategies, but work in fieldwork sites and other research indicate that there was rarely *any* attempt to apply a systematic approach to learning.

80. In one area, the local police commander described the local process of strategy development as 'initiative chasing', where partner agencies placed more importance on 'show' projects than on having a sound basis for such work. An analysis of 335 multi-agency community safety initiatives by the Police Research Group for HM Inspectorate of Constabulary (HMIC) found that very few had applied analytical, problem-solving processes **[EXHIBIT 16]**.

EXHIBIT 16

Evaluation of community safety initiatives

HMIC found that few multi-agency community safety initiatives stood up to scrutiny.

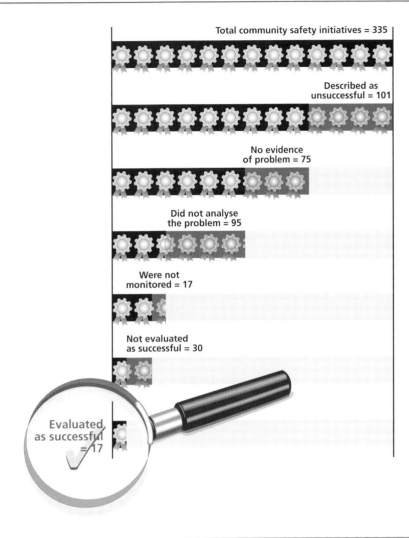

Source: Beating Crime, HMIC (Ref. 39)

81. Fieldwork interviews supported the conclusion that staff often felt pressed – for example, by strong public or member support – into adopting particular projects that were not be the best solution to the problem in hand. One community safety co-ordinator commented that he spent as much of his time dissuading the organisation from pursuing initiatives that were unlikely to solve a particular problem as he did on devising and supporting new initiatives. A police commander described how a local district council had proposed an 'alley-gating' project (in which people on community service orders constructed gates to protect the back of Victorian houses from being used as 'rat runs') because they had seen one in a neighbouring authority, despite the fact that they did not have the same type of housing in the district. Much of the current work on community safety may be at best poorly targeted, and at worst wasted effort.

82. In part, the failure to evaluate 'what works' can be attributed to growing media and public pressure to see more 'bobbies on the beat' and CCTV as solutions to the problems of community insecurity. Such calls

The lack of a common skills and knowledge base for community safety work has been hindering progress

have formed the rationale for quite significant investments in strategies that experience suggests are unlikely to solve particular local problems. Some authorities have responded to these calls by appointing civic guards and/or installing cameras but, usually, it has not been possible to demonstrate the effectiveness of these initiatives. The new Crime and Disorder Act provides a number of new tools for agencies – such as community safety orders and child curfew schemes – that could be viewed by the public as panaceas for local problems. The new partnerships will need to examine such assumptions and ensure that these tools are used only where appropriate, and where they offer the best solution.

83. There is a need for staff with the time and appropriate skills to draw on existing research to inform strategic choices about community safety. While some co-ordinators have become adept at networking and sharing best practice, the lack of a common skills and knowledge base for community safety work has been hindering progress. The range of awareness of 'what works' within fieldwork sites was very wide – many co-ordinators were unaware of key research published nationally, or of how to find out where such expertise might exist.

84. Of the fieldwork strategies reviewed, three had conducted an authority-wide audit that was then used as a basis for prioritising further community safety work. But in many cases, partnerships had simply created a 'laundry list' of community safety strategies in which the rationale for the choice of projects was unclear [**EXHIBIT 17**].

EXHIBIT 17

An example of a community safety strategy predating the Act

In some cases, there was a 'laundry list' approach to community safety work in which the rationale for the choice of projects was unclear.

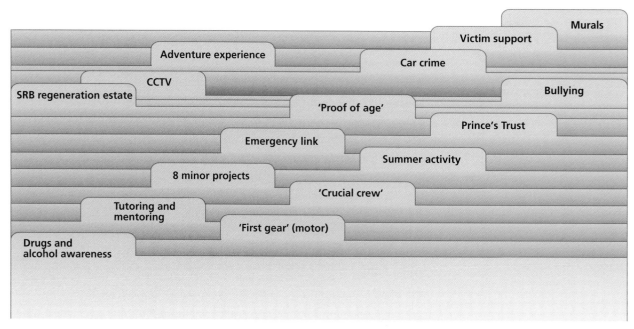

Source: Audit Commission fieldwork

The absence of a link between the audit and strategies made it very difficult for partnerships to learn and develop

Monitoring and evaluation

85. With so many community safety initiatives unconnected to a baseline audit, it was difficult to set informed targets for work and to monitor and evaluate any subsequent progress. Monitoring and evaluation are essential tools for learning what is (or is not) working in the adopted strategy. The absence of a link between the audit and strategies therefore made it very difficult for partnerships to learn and develop.

86. But the absence of a link between an audit and community safety strategies was not the only problem. Many projects were not monitored due to lack of time (often the community safety co-ordinator was the only person with this responsibility); and/or an inability to provide statistics (especially where one agency required statistics from another – for example, the police were the only ones able to track the impact of a youth project, but could not collate statistics on the relevant geographic area); and/or lack of resources to conduct surveys (for example, a fear of crime survey was conducted to provide a baseline but the resources to re-survey to measure the impact of the intervention were subsequently withdrawn due to budget pressures).

87. Even where resources were made available, evaluations were all too often post hoc, with no baseline against which to compare progress; or lacked provisions to track any displacement of problems to other areas; and/or did not track sustainable progress. At worst, this situation resulted in a syndrome of constant 'crackdown' initiatives, with positive results reported that were not sustained. The lack of a problem-solving approach prompted two academics to describe the field of community safety as *'dominated by self-serving unpublished and semi-published work that does not meet even the most elementary criteria of evaluative probity'* (Ref. 45).

88. National-level performance indicators do not currently reflect the re-emphasis from crime to community safety. For example, police forces still feel under pressure to increase detections per officer rather than to reduce crime, which is harder to attribute. More significantly, national statistics are not signalling to non-police agencies – such as education authorities and social services – that they, too, need to focus on safety issues and should be held to account for the impact of their work on crime and fear of crime.

89. The provisions in the Crime and Disorder Act for each partnership to conduct authority-wide audits, publish an analysis of those audits and to monitor and evaluate strategies, are welcome requirements in this developing field. However, evidence to date suggests that authorities have a long way to go ensure that the best use is made of public funds that are invested in promoting community safety. In particular, a greater understanding of the causes of, and solutions to, local community safety problems is needed to ensure that the work is well targeted.

Under-investment in prevention

90. Having identified priority areas for community safety work, a strategy should set out an intended response and how it will be resourced. In common with other types of preventative work, community safety is a difficult area in which to identify or measure the need for resources. This issue is common to other government-inspired, problem-solving approaches (Ref. 46).

91. Major obstacles to investing in community safety are:

• under-developed cost-benefit thinking;

• difficulties with identifying budgets in the first place; and

• insufficient investment in people to do this new work.

Underdeveloped cost-benefit thinking

92. The Crime and Disorder Act encourages partners to look for 'win-win' investments in prevention, which actually save money. But, in practice, not all partners are convinced that community safety will pay back their investment or that the savings will accrue to them quickly enough to justify their investment. This scepticism has led to a 'part-time' approach to community safety, where staff have been asked to do community safety work in addition to their core duties.

93. Perhaps unsurprisingly, community safety has in the past suffered from a dependency on fundraising, with authorities trying to identify external funds wherever possible for what has until recently been non-statutory work. Consequently, the funding of community safety has relied on the skill and ingenuity of policy and community safety officers to raise funds from any sources that they could find. Such effort was often costly: in one site, 30 officers in a chief executive's department were employed largely in administering external bids for regeneration and other activities linked to community safety. Those authorities that were able to identify expenditure revealed a complex funding 'cocktail' **[EXHIBIT 18]**.

94. While central government and other grant-givers have tried to promote community safety work in the past, complex funding streams are difficult and time-consuming to administer. Furthermore, dependency on external fundraising makes community safety work vulnerable – the possibility that funding may be withdrawn makes sustainability a major issue. Exit strategies are needed when an approach is so dependent on funding initiatives. Such strategies were not apparent, and staff on local projects felt vulnerable as a result. Precarious funding also has the unwanted effect of keeping community safety apart from mainstream services within agencies. The effects of this are discussed later in this chapter.

95. A reliance on external funds, or very marginal funding from mainstream budgets, to pay for community safety work is unlikely to be enough. Partnerships are not routinely using a cost-benefit approach and so are not able to quantify either the costs of community safety problems or the potential savings that could be achieved by investing from their own resources.

EXHIBIT 18

Funding sources for separate budgets for community safety – local authorities

Those authorities able to identify expenditure revealed a complex funding 'cocktail'.

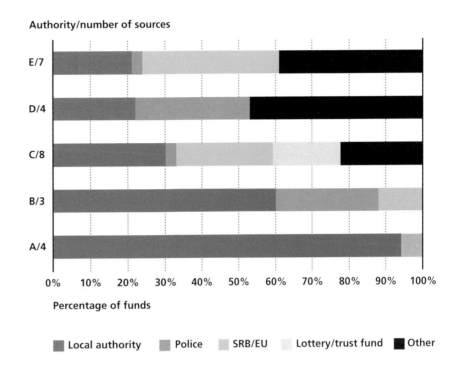

Authority/number of sources

Percentage of funds

■ Local authority ■ Police ▨ SRB/EU ▨ Lottery/trust fund ■ Other

Source: Audit Commission fieldwork

96. Few fieldwork sites had undertaken sufficient work on costing the community safety problems in their area to make the case for investing in initiatives to reduce those costs. Four out of ten had commissioned studies by Crime Concern on the costs of crime in their area, but this work was rarely sustained – as systems were not developed to update the figures or track any reductions achieved. Where authorities have done work on costing crime, the approaches that they have used are not comparable. For example, some authorities have measured costs to businesses and private individuals; others have measured the costs of specific crimes **[EXHIBIT 19]**.

EXHIBIT 19

Examples of costing of crime

Some authorities have done work on costing crime locally, but their approaches are not comparable.

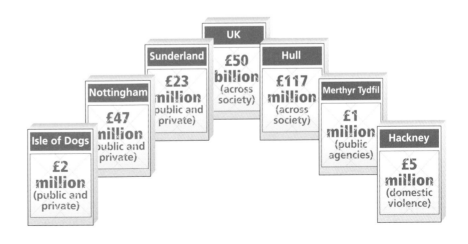

Source: Crime Concern; London Borough of Hackney (Ref. 29); Hull City Council (Ref. 30)

97. In summary, community safety work has tended to rely on a fundraising approach, bypassing mainstream budgets and consequently receiving a low priority. Cost-benefit approaches remain underdeveloped but are badly needed to make the case for further investment by partner agencies in community safety.

Difficulties with identifying budgets

98. Only one of the strategies reviewed actually identified a specific budget for its community safety work. This was an arm's-length partnership which operated as a limited company and was required to produce an annual report. The absence of funding statements represents a major shortcoming in accountability. When asked about resourcing, only six out of the ten local authority sites were able to identify a separate budget for community safety – in five out of these six cases it was a seedcorn budget, which amounted to less than 0.2 per cent of the local authority's total revenue budget. This position accords with the national picture, which showed that in March 1998 only a minority of local authorities and police forces had a separate budget of greater than £100,000 per year [EXHIBIT 20].

EXHIBIT 20

Size of separate budgets for community safety

A minority of local authorities and police forces had a separate budget of greater than £100,000 per year.

Percentage of respondents

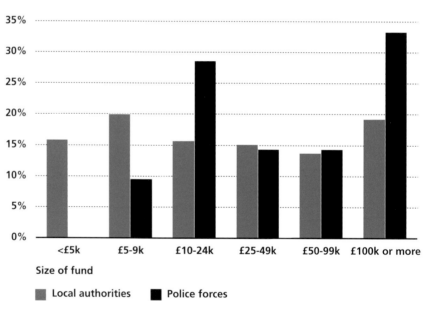

Size of fund

■ Local authorities ■ Police forces

Source: Universities of Liverpool and Huddersfield Survey (Ref. 39)

99. To put this in perspective, even in the context of the smallest authorities, budgets below £100,000 would be considered to be relatively small. In 1997/98, the average shire police force budget in England and Wales was £98 million; the average shire district council budget was £15 million (Ref. 47) and so, where separate budgets existed, community safety spending represented well below 1 per cent of each organisation's expenditure.

100. Staff in fieldwork sites explained that such budgets were used to 'pump-prime' community safety work in other parts of the authority. However, the level of activity that took place as a result of these funds, and the outcomes, were not tracked. Because it was not budgeted for as part of mainstream work, the full range of community safety activity was not accounted for and therefore remained invisible to partnerships. Partnerships were unable to track the cost-effectiveness of different interventions, and some wasted money on untested approaches.

101. Furthermore, financial regulations within local agencies can increase the disincentives to be explicit about funding. For example, funds cannot be taken from a local authority housing revenue account to pay for schemes to divert young people from crime, although this might effectively reduce the repair bill for the housing department in the long run. Once budgets are set, they can rarely be transferred for other purposes. The difficulty in aligning budgets with outcomes is a major obstacle to ensuring the effective use of public funds spent on community safety.

Insufficient investment in people

102. In addition to budgeting for community safety, authorities are increasingly appointing staff to posts that cover this new work. A recent survey found that, by March 1998, most local authorities had at least one member of staff with a community safety remit, although that person often had responsibilities beyond community safety [EXHIBIT 21].

103. Job descriptions and person specifications for these posts varied widely. There were considerable differences in the grading, role and activities performed by local authority community safety officers, with posts varying from relatively junior operational staff to senior managers. Roles included anything from policy development to direct project management, with activities embracing emergency planning, fundraising and training. A review by the national network of community safety co-ordinators highlighted a number of development needs for the staff in post [EXHIBIT 22, overleaf]. It also showed that staff ranked developing and maintaining community safety strategies as their top priority, with empowering the community the lowest.

EXHIBIT 21

Full time staff for community safety

Most authorities had at least one person in post.

Number of staff (% local authorities)

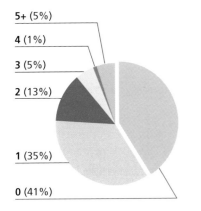

5+ (5%)
4 (1%)
3 (5%)
2 (13%)
1 (35%)
0 (41%)

Source: University of Liverpool and Huddersfield Survey (Ref. 39)

EXHIBIT 22

Profile of local authority community safety co-ordinators

A review by the national network of community safety co-ordinators highlighted a number of development needs for the staff in post.

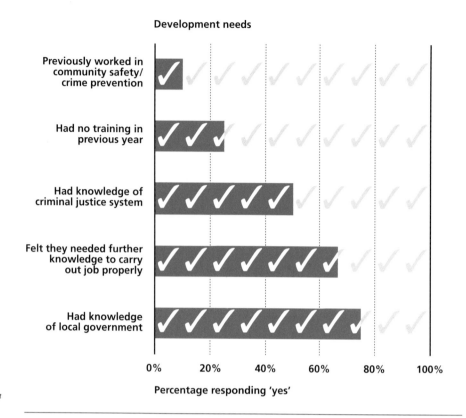

Development needs

- Previously worked in community safety/ crime prevention
- Had no training in previous year
- Had knowledge of criminal justice system
- Felt they needed further knowledge to carry out job properly
- Had knowledge of local government

0% 20% 40% 60% 80% 100%

Percentage responding 'yes'

Source: National Network of Community Safety Co-ordinators in England – based on sample of 42 returns, March 1998

104. During the course of the Audit Commission's research, several authorities reported vacant posts, long-term illness and problems with recruiting staff into post. Across one region covering three counties in the south east of England, 40 per cent of posts were vacant. In another region, there was poaching of skilled and experienced staff between authorities. The recent extent of adverts in the national press provides evidence of the difficulties in recruiting to community safety posts.

105. Police forces experienced particular difficulties in identifying staff working on community safety, since this forms an integral part of their daily work. Nonetheless, the need to develop a cadre of 'problem-solvers' and to recruit officers suited to partnership working in order to ensure the proper resourcing of community safety work was still evident. In particular, policies of tenure of post often made it difficult for police officers to acquire expertise and credibility in partnership work.

106. Training in community safety work has also been patchy. At the national level, the Home Office runs a Crime Prevention College to train police officers in this area, but fieldwork sites found the absence of appropriate training across partnerships, and of national standards to underpin this training, a problem.

Staffing for community safety did not always reflect the needs of the partnership

107. Partnerships will need to give careful thought to the skills required both to develop community safety strategies and to deliver these locally. The skills of a co-ordinator, who may be charged with negotiating with directors of large service departments and 'brokering' solutions to community safety work, are quite different from those needed by a policy officer, who requires a sharp appreciation of the causes of problems and what works in tackling them. A local manager working closely with community groups to encourage people to confront local problems would need different skills again.

108. Finally, staffing for community safety did not always reflect the needs of the partnership. Effective joint working requires strong links between each agency at all levels of the organisation: strategic, joint policy analysis and operational. Few partnerships had reflected this need in their partnership infrastructure, and difficulties in deciding who should follow up on work outside the partnership meetings were observed as a result.

Unclear rationale for partnership

109. The rationale for setting up a partnership for community safety has not always been clear. Setting up a partnership has at times been viewed as a community safety initiative in its own right. A recent Audit Commission management paper commented on progress with partnership working across a number of services (Ref. 48). Working in partnership is relatively new, and the work of partnerships reviewed for this study was, to a large extent, pioneering. The key problems faced by partnerships were:

- difficulty in establishing clear ownership of and accountability for action; and
- complex links in the delivery of strategies.

Ownership and accountability

110. A number of different forms of partnership were observed in fieldwork sites. Some had been in place since the early 1990s; others had come together for the express purpose of seeking external funding, such as Safer Cities or SRB funding. Some were led by one agency (often the police), whilst others existed at police force or county level. One review of 114 existing strategies found that the documentation of work was generally poor and that most strategies were really action plans or structures of organisations put together as exit strategies for Safer Cities schemes, rather than a statement of priorities and how they would be achieved (Ref. 49). Therefore, a tendency for discussions to be about the form and structure of partnerships, and not their purpose, was still hindering progress.

Community safety was seen by health authorities as a low priority

111. All partnerships in the study had representation from police and local government, but the range of agencies covered often went much wider than the current requirements of the Crime and Disorder Act, as outlined in Appendix 1 [EXHIBIT 23].

112. There were major difficulties in encouraging health service representatives to attend meetings. The failure of health authority staff to participate in, or be able to commit their organisations to, community safety strategies illustrated the fact that community safety was seen by health authorities as a low priority. In general, there was difficulty in making a case that health partners would benefit from contributing to such strategies, especially at a time of considerable change within the NHS.

113. By contrast, the Crime and Disorder Act does not stipulate that fire brigades must work in partnership with other agencies, despite the fact that in many places they already participate. The risk factors linked to being the victim of fire accidents and crime are broadly similar and situated in similar communities (Ref. 50), and tackling issues of fire safety in a community safety partnership would seem a natural opportunity for 'win-win' solutions. This was the experience in Merseyside, where the Safer Merseyside Partnership was able to use problem-solving approaches developed for community safety to save fire brigade resources by tackling the problem of hoax callers, which accounted for 25 per cent of calls to the brigade.

EXHIBIT 23

Current progress with partnerships

The range of agencies participating in partnerships reviewed by this study often went much wider than the current requirements of the Crime and Disorder Act.

Site	Date formed	Local authority	Police	Police authority	Probation	Health	Private sector	Voluntary sector	Public	Fire
		REQUIRED BY THE ACT								
A	1994	✓	✓	✓	✓	✓	✓	✓	✗	✓
B	1992	✓	✓	✗	✓	✓	✓	✓	✗	✓
C	1994	✓	✓	✗	✓	✗	✓	✓	✓	✓
D	1994	✓/✗	✓	✗	✓	✓	✗	✓	✗	✗
E	1993	✓/✗	✓	✗	✗	★	✗	✗	✓	✗
F	1996	✓	✓	✗	✓	★	✗	✗	✗	✗
G	1992	✓	✓	✗	✗	✗	✓	✓	✗	✗
H	1997	✓	✓	✓	✓	✓	✗	✗	✗	✗
I	1995	✓	✓	✗	✓	Trust	✗	✓	✓	✗
J	1990	✓	✓	✗	✓	✗	✓	✓	✗	✗

★ 'On and off' or at project working group level

✓/✗ Where a county and district structure exists but only one tier is in the partnership

Source: Audit Commission fieldwork

Another key challenge is to recognise the differences in the culture and working styles of partner organisations

114. In many areas a major challenge for partnerships continues to be the lack of coterminous boundaries between agencies. It is quite common for a police force command unit, a district council, health authority and operational areas within a county council all to have different geographical boundaries. This makes it difficult to identify which agencies should be in the partnership in the first place, let alone have a common 'map' for deciding priorities and objectives and subsequently tracking activity and outcomes in relation to problems.

115. Another key challenge is to recognise the differences in the culture and working styles of partner organisations. The staff who sat on partnerships often encountered problems with lack of continuity or lack of ability of those around the table to commit their organisations. For example, many police forces operate a policy of rotating staff in specialist posts, which makes it difficult to achieve continuity in police personnel on partnerships.

116. One of the main criticisms levelled at partnership working has been the lack of accountability for action and the risk of partnerships becoming 'talking shops' (Ref. 51). In many sites visited for this study it was difficult to find clear documentary evidence of actions that had been decided at partnership meetings. Strategy documents were rarely of sufficient detail to identify lead responsibilities, targets and review dates.

Links to local delivery

117. Few strategies identified a clear, accountable link between the strategy and local delivery of community safety work. And where people had thought through links, they were often complex. At one site there was a complex web of reporting lines back to the strategy group, which made it very difficult for people within the 'web' to see how their work related to other parts of the partnership [EXHIBIT 24].

118. This complexity could result in staff on local projects feeling somewhat insecure and isolated. Uncertainty over future funding meant that many projects lacked support from mainstream agencies. Staff were typically seconded or brought in on short-term contracts. While many local projects had the potential to develop new and innovative ways of working, they often lacked the support needed to make them sustainable or capable of being rolled out throughout the organisation. Some of the best links between partnerships and local delivery were seen in SRB projects, where it was a requirement of funding that accountability systems were set up with named managers and links to departmental plans. However, this attention to process was not observed where the requirements were not so tightly specified.

EXHIBIT 24

Reporting lines between partnership and local delivery in one fieldwork site

There was a complex web of reporting lines back to one strategy group.

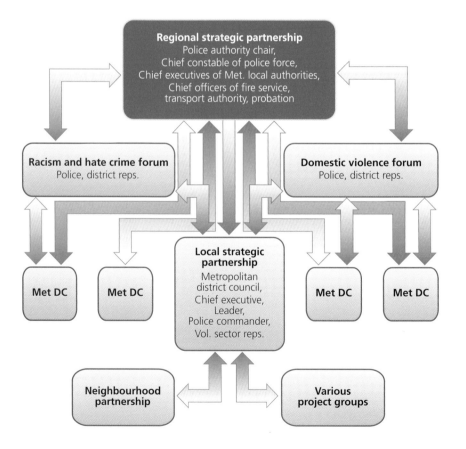

Source: Audit Commission fieldwork site

46

Lack of integration with mainstream public services

This lack of a corporate approach is currently the single biggest barrier to the successful development of community safety

119. A problem with much partnership work is that the partners may be asked to take action that they may not directly benefit from themselves. In other words, incentives are not aligned with the capacity to act to prevent community safety problems. For example, to address youth disorder or nuisance, a local authority may invest in a youth centre, which reduces calls to the police, or the police may increase the level of visible patrol and reduce the costs of vandalism and neighbour nuisance for the local authority housing department. In each case, the costs fall on one partner but benefits also accrue to another. Generating ownership of community safety has thus been difficult.

120. Once a partnership has evaluated the options for delivering community safety, the approach in the past has typically been to set up individual projects to address identified community safety problems that have been managed separately from agencies' mainstream activities. Agency departments have been neither invited nor required to take part in an integrated approach to promoting community safety. Encouraging mainstream departments to participate unlocks the resource base of participating agencies. This lack of a corporate approach is currently the single biggest barrier to the successful development of community safety. Moreover, the lack of a coherent local approach results in inconsistent services being delivered on the ground for local people. This lack of an integrated corporate approach was seen most clearly in:

- an undeveloped understanding of what individual agencies might be able to contribute and how;

- the difficulty in integrating community safety into crowded corporate agendas; and

- an emphasis on situational approaches to safety, and less emphasis on addressing the causes of offending behaviour.

Understanding how each agency might contribute

121. In interviews for this study, individual departments within agencies were usually keen to point out what their department was doing to address community safety. However, departmental plans rarely named community safety as a priority. Sites were invariably unable to produce an inventory of work going on among and between departments, and so a complete overview could not be compiled. One partnership reviewed the work of its partners and found that much was already happening that may not currently be viewed as community safety or targeted at community safety problems but which, once identified, could lead to greater synergy of effort [EXHIBIT 25, overleaf].

122. If only to comply with Section 17 of the Crime and Disorder Act, which requires partner agencies to take into account the community safety implications of their existing work, authorities will need to be more rigorous in cataloguing such activity, thinking through the boundary issues between different activities and considering the coherence of their overall effort in contributing to positive community safety outcomes.

EXHIBIT 25

Examples of work related to community safety within key partner agencies

Much is already happening within partner agencies that may not currently be viewed as community safety or targeted at community safety problems but which, once identified, can contribute to greater synergy of effort.

	Police	Local Authority	Fire Service	Probation	Health
Community/ Neighbourhood	Community officers Neighbourhood watch	Racism and harassment Noise and nuisance Resident involvement	Smoke alarms	Community service	Health promotion
Family	Child protection	Family centres Child protection		Family court welfare	Family centres
Young People	Schools liaison	Children's plans Drugs education Youth work CAMHS*	Fire safety education	YOT** members	Drugs education
Individuals at risk	YOT** members Reprimands Warnings	YOT** members Excluded pupils Community care	Arson Hoax calls	YOT** members Adult justice Rehabilitation of offenders	YOT** members Community care Drug treatment
Victims	Victim's charter Referrals to Victim Support Domestic violence	Vulnerable adults Domestic violence		Release of high risk offenders Domestic violence	Domestic violence Victims of assault

* Child and adolescent mental health services

** Youth offending teams

Source: Adapted from work done by the Thames Valley Partnership

Crowded corporate agendas

123. A further strategic challenge for partnerships will be the integration of community safety into busy corporate agendas. Much community safety work is linked to other existing and new developments [EXHIBIT 26]. All policy decisions will have to take into account the community safety implications, requiring consistent links to be made to other plans. To date, community safety has not been integrated with other corporate work so this requirement will be a major challenge for partner agencies.

124. Of these, two areas in particular – youth crime and drugs – are so closely linked that it is worth considering their integration as a priority. Crime committed by people under 18 accounts for around one-quarter of offences (Ref. 52); recent research in a number of areas has suggested that over 60 per cent of those arrested by the police have traces of illegal drugs in their urine (Ref. 53). Since drugs and youth crime are highly likely to feature in many community safety strategies, a co-ordinated approach is particularly important between strategies to address community safety, drugs and youth offending.

125. The two organisations covering these closely linked areas are the new youth offending teams (YOTs), which must be in place by April 2000 but are already beginning to form, and the existing drugs action teams (DATs or DAATs – drugs and alcohol action teams – in Wales). The memberships of these three groups have significant overlap, and some authorities' staff are going from one meeting to another, discussing broadly similar agendas, but with little co-ordination at either the strategic or delivery level.

EXHIBIT 26

Community safety – links to other corporate initiatives

Much of community safety is linked to other new and existing developments.

Source: Audit Commission

Situational emphasis

126. Successful strategies address not only community safety problems but also their causes. There are three broad types of approach to tackling community safety (Ref. 54):

- *enforcement* (for example, tenancy enforcement, policing, and other criminal justice interventions);

- *situational* (addressing environmental risks to communities through physical alterations to buildings and the environment); and

- *social* (dealing with offending behaviour and its causes).

127. If community safety programmes fail to balance the short-term addressing of a problem with longer-term, sustainable solutions, then they risk not using public money effectively. One way of gauging the relative importance currently placed by partnerships on these measures is to look at the relative spend on each. This reveals an overwhelming emphasis on situational measures, suggesting that a balanced approach is not in place [EXHIBIT 27]. Situational investment has its place but, because its results are tangible, it can dominate strategies at the expense of equally valid and important enforcement and social projects.

EXHIBIT 27

Relative funding emphasis on different approaches in fieldwork sites

In fieldwork sites an overwhelming emphasis on situational measures was found, suggesting that a balanced approach was not in place.

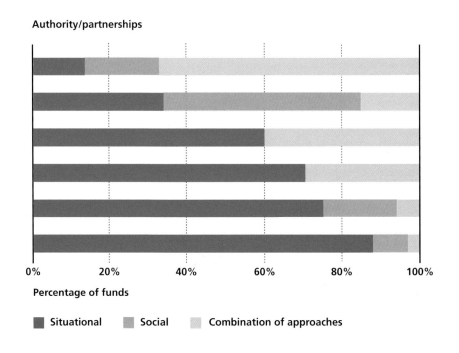

Authority/partnerships

Percentage of funds

■ Situational   ■ Social   ■ Combination of approaches

Source: Audit Commission fieldwork

128. Staff in fieldwork sites cited pressures to adopt situational approaches including the fact that grant regimes (for example, CCTV challenge funds) often encourage them; situational measures were easier to 'sell' to politicians and to the public because they were more visible; and they were easier to evaluate, since their effects were often more immediate. Social measures – such as detached youth work and parenting classes – often take years to show results, and so were harder to evaluate. One fieldwork site undertook a more detailed analysis of the funding sources for community safety and the uses to which those funds were put. This analysis revealed that external funding may well have distorted local priorities and contributed to an emphasis on situational measures [**EXHIBIT 28**].

129. But an analysis of partnership budgets alone is not sufficient evidence from which to draw firm conclusions. All sites mentioned activities that were being provided through mainstream budgets but were not considered to be part of community safety. This would be particularly true of resources for enforcement, which come from mainstream policing and housing budgets. Other examples included education welfare, housing improvements and the council youth service. However, even if a comprehensive stock-take of budgets reveals a more balanced picture, the dispersal of such spending across the functions of partner agencies reduces clarity over resources and inhibits a properly 'joined-up' corporate approach.

EXHIBIT 28

Comparison of sources and use of funds in one fieldwork site

External funding may well have promoted an emphasis on situational measures.

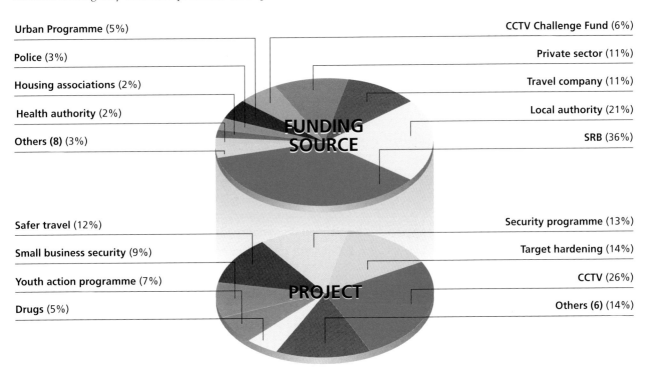

Urban Programme (5%)

Police (3%)

Housing associations (2%)

Health authority (2%)

Others (8) (3%)

CCTV Challenge Fund (6%)

Private sector (11%)

Travel company (11%)

Local authority (21%)

SRB (36%)

FUNDING SOURCE

Safer travel (12%)

Small business security (9%)

Youth action programme (7%)

Drugs (5%)

Security programme (13%)

Target hardening (14%)

CCTV (26%)

Others (6) (14%)

PROJECT

Source: Audit Commission fieldwork site

130. Moreover, a corporate approach would allow for considerable emphasis on social approaches to community safety, drawing on the experience of education, social services and health authorities. For example, promising approaches to community safety include family support services, parenting classes and pre-school education, but these services cannot be provided without the co-operation of the major mainstream agencies.

131. To achieve a corporate approach, changes are required at all levels of government. In preparation for the Crime and Disorder Act, central government departments have not reviewed how their top-down objectives square with a bottom-up, outcome-focused approach.

132. The lack of a national performance regime to track progress of the Act's implementation across all government services exemplifies this problem. Since the Home Office leads on the Act, it is well placed to develop a range of measures. But agencies that need to be held to account for community safety activities, such as local authorities and NHS agencies, relate to other central government departments, and a cross-cutting basket of measures that promotes partnership working and a focus on outcomes across different agencies has not yet been developed to support the Act.

133. Finally, the Government could usefully provide greater assurance that the mixed economy of providers of enforcement and crime prevention services is suitably regulated. For example, the increasing use of non-police uniformed patrol, such as civic guards, and CCTV cameras, poses questions about whether the public is sufficiently protected from inappropriate people becoming involved in this work.

Conclusion

134. Community safety in many areas is not a 'greenfield' site. Statutory agencies have already made significant moves in the field of community safety within existing resources. In particular, many have formed local partnerships that have laid useful foundations. The Crime and Disorder Act places a new emphasis on this work, but will it solve the current shortcomings? The evidence of a sound basis for much of the past work of these partnerships, or of sufficient resources to match their intentions is not clear, prompting questions about the effectiveness of future work. In particular, stronger links to local delivery will be needed, together with a greater emphasis on performance management and learning from what does and does not work. This last chapter has detailed the problems with approaches to date on community safety [EXHIBIT 29]; the next chapter aims to provide a set of solutions to the problems based on current best practice.

EXHIBIT 29

Community safety – problems and causes

This chapter has identified the key problems facing those working on community safety and explored their underlying causes.

Problems	Causes
Poor grounding in local people's views 	• Failure to give sufficient weight to local views • Failure to develop an overall communications strategy • Difficulty in reconciling bottom-up and top-down views
Poor grasp of causes of and solutions to community safety problems	• Insufficiently thorough mapping and analysis of problems • Lack of understanding of 'what works' • Insufficient monitoring and evaluation
Under-investment in prevention	• Reliance on external funding • Difficulty in identifying spending on community safety • Under-investment in people
Unclear rationale for partnership	• Difficulty in establishing clear ownership and accountability • Complex reporting links to delivery
Lack of integration of community safety with mainstream agencies 	• Mainstream agencies and departments do not see relevance to their work • Crowded corporate agendas • Emphasis on situational project approaches bypassing mainstream departments

Source: Audit Commission

3

Promising Approaches to Promoting Community Safety

A more concerted approach to promoting community safety is needed by public agencies to reflect local people's priorities. The new partnerships need to engage better with local communities, invest in what works and learn from what does not. Finally, community safety needs to be viewed by mainstream services as part of their work.

135. The previous chapter identified five major challenges for the new statutory partnerships, drawing on lessons from partnerships and strategies that have already been developed prior to the Crime and Disorder Act. Rising to these challenges will not be an overnight exercise, and will require a 'step-change' in approach from all involved, including those with strategies that pre-date the Act.

136. However, a number of partnerships have overcome some of the obstacles identified in Chapter 2. This chapter aims to offer solutions to the problems based on current best practice. Anyone looking for a simple recipe to apply locally will be disappointed. Community safety is classed as a 'wicked' issue for a good reason. The solutions are elusive and complex, not obvious and simple. What is needed is a learning approach within which there must be as much willingness to identify projects that fail as to celebrate success.

137. The solutions to the challenges of community safety mirror the problems, and are described in turn. Effective strategies need to:

- engage with local communities;
- develop a learning approach to community safety;
- develop an investment approach to community safety;
- develop accountable and delivery-focused partnerships; and
- integrate community safety into the mainstream [**EXHIBIT 30**].

EXHIBIT 30

The solutions to the challenges of community safety

This chapter discusses the five main solutions that mirror the problems of community safety.

Effective strategies need to...

...engage with local communities

...develop a learning approach to community safety

...develop an investment approach to community safety

...develop accountable and delivery-focused partnerships

...integrate community safety into the mainstream

Source: Audit Commission

Engaging with local communities

138. Partnerships need to take stock of existing consultation mechanisms and develop a coherent communications strategy to ensure that key groups are identified and heard. In some cases, a concerted approach to developing groups that would not otherwise feel able to engage with partnership agencies is needed.

Developing a communications strategy

139. A community safety communications strategy should aim for a two-way dialogue, asking people what makes them feel unsafe and what might address the problem. In developing a communications strategy, partnerships must form a view of what they want to communicate and to whom, and then choose a method. In effect, the consultation approach should be tailored to the purpose of the exercise, and could span a spectrum from simply making people aware of what the partnership is doing through to engaging with people and ultimately giving them a real say in what should be done [**EXHIBIT 31**].

140. Clearly the more intensive the mechanisms, the more costly they are. Partnerships will need to strike a balance between:

- wide coverage, identifying strategic issues for people across an authority; and

- focused consultation with 'hard-to-reach' groups on issues that require further analysis with local people.

EXHIBIT 31

Purpose of consultation and corresponding methods

The consultation approach should be tailored to the purpose of the exercise.

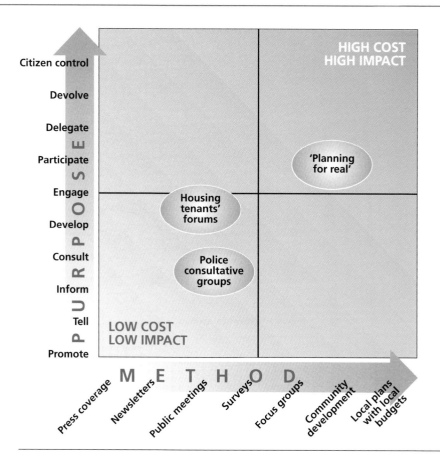

Source: Audit Commission

141. Of particular importance within the communications strategy will be managing the local media. The best partnerships were aware of the effects of uninformed or adverse publicity and had strong links with the local press and media. Such a relationship cannot be taken for granted – some partnerships have had difficult relations with their local press. However, in two fieldwork sites, the editor of the local paper was actually a participating member of the community safety partnership.

142. Schemes such as Neighbourhood Watch and Home Watch can be a useful means of involving local people in areas where volunteers wish to come forward, but these have waned in number since the early 1990s. While they can be effective in promoting surveillance and generating community confidence, they are less easy to form in high-crime areas. They are therefore unlikely in the short term to form the main focus of a strategy aimed at reducing crime.

143. Partnerships need to review not only which groups they want to reach, but what they are already doing to reach them. As a starting point, they should audit their mechanisms for communication. This will enable them to identify gaps and duplication in existing approaches, as a basis for developing an overall communications strategy on community safety. Such an approach has been successful in Bradford [CASE STUDY 1, overleaf].

144. A number of mechanisms exist that bring together the different strands of community safety. Northampton has multi-agency forums for consulting specifically on community safety, attended by professionals from the various different agencies. Basildon has organised its consultation through nine joint estate management committees. These committees include residents and representatives from local agencies that work on the estates.

CASE STUDY 1

City of Bradford Metropolitan District Council's approach to public consultation

Background

To prepare for its community plan as well as its best value pilot on community safety, Bradford has undertaken a review of its consultation mechanisms. The authority was aware that current mechanisms did not cover all groups that it wished to reach, yet risked over-surveying others.

Action and results

In developing its community plan (1997-2000), the council conducted its largest ever public consultation exercise and found that over half the respondents stressed the crucial importance of tackling crime and fear of crime.

As part of its strategy for being closer to its communities, the authority developed the Area Panels Initiative, which consists of five area panels based on five parliamentary constituencies within the Bradford District. A network of neighbourhood forums underpin the work of the area panels, with 77 neighbourhood forums across the district. These forums give local people a voice while providing the council with an effective consultation mechanism, and they have been used to give feedback on community safety concerns.

The council also has a 'speak-out' panel of 2,500 local residents, which is statistically representative of local communities. This panel is surveyed regularly on various 'hot topics,' one of which has been community safety.

For the crime and disorder audits, the council worked closely with the police to identify various 'hard-to-reach' groups – such as young people and Asian women – and consulted them using different mechanisms. To consult young people, the council engaged other young people and the Youth Service to access groups of young people in the district (a peer-led approach); Asian women were consulted via focus groups and using a bilingual mediator. In addition, over 200 public, private and voluntary sector agencies were consulted using semi-structured questionnaires and pro formas.

All of these approaches, taken together, have been used to inform both the best value pilot and the crime and disorder audit.

Good practice points

- the council reviewed existing consultation mechanisms to spot gaps and duplication;

- it developed a locally based network of consultation groups to allow ease of access for local people;

- it had an overall strategy for communicating with local people, tailoring different methods to different purposes; and

- the approach adopted linked consultation and strategy development.

In some areas a more concerted effort may be needed to encourage a dialogue on community safety

Supporting key groups in high-crime areas

145. To date, authorities have found that convential consultation methods, such as surveys or public meetings, have failed to reach those most in need. In some areas a more concerted effort may be needed to encourage a dialogue on community safety. This can be particularly important in high-crime areas, where:

- witness intimidation frequently occurs, discouraging people from identifying local offenders for fear of reprisal; and

- fear of crime is a key concern to local residents, often rendering them housebound.

146. Such concerted approaches take considerable time and effort and cannot and should not be conducted everywhere. They should be targeted on small areas where partnerships believe that there is a strong but perhaps silent concern about community safety. Methods such as *Planning for Real* and engaging in community development can be used to make contact with excluded groups [CASE STUDY 2].

CASE STUDY 2

Planning for Real in Basildon

Background

After a lengthy consultation period, Basildon District Council, in partnership with the Anglia Housing Group, transferred ownership of an estate in East Basildon to Vange Community Housing, a new local housing company. The transfer of 700 council-owned properties took place under the Government's Estate Renewal Challenge Fund initiative. It will enable the Anglia Housing Group to invest £25 million in the physical fabric of tenants' homes and the environmental appearance of the estate.

The estate experiences some of the worst deprivation in the district, with high levels of unemployment and crime, poor health and low achievement at school. Basildon Council and the Anglia Housing Group recognised that, for the physical transformation of the estate to be successful, it would be necessary to develop a community plan to address the issues of deprivation and social exclusion. This plan would need to engage positively with local people.

Action and results

In April 1998, Basildon Council, the Anglia Housing Group, Essex County Council and the South Essex Area Health Authority hosted two *Planning for Real* events on the estate. The events were facilitated by the Neighbourhood Initiatives Foundation.

continued overleaf...

CASE STUDY 2 (cont.)

Action and results (cont.)

To generate ownership of the project, a scale model of the estate was built by local school children. Residents were invited to place cards on the model to identify the type and location of problems that they were experiencing and their suggested solutions to these problems. The response by residents was very positive, with 1,220 cards being placed on the model by over 200 residents. An analysis of the cards showed that:

- 36 per cent were related to community safety (including youth disorder, streetlighting and calls for additional police patrols);

- 16 per cent related to the environment (including tree planting, dog fouling and litter); and

- 15 per cent related to traffic and transport problems (particularly requests for traffic calming measures).

Other cards covered job creation and training, leisure and community facilities and healthy living.

Good practice points

- the council recognised the need to use intensive mechanisms for consulting with groups in an area where people were less likely to come forward;

- *Planning for Real* enabled public agencies to involve local people and generate ownership for the work; and

- involving local people generated an expectation of action for staff in public agencies and a sense of purposeful intervention for those staff.

147. Particular problems can arise with crimes that tend not to be reported to public agencies. Innovative approaches to specific problems, such as witness intimidation, have been developed in a number of areas. The London Borough of Newham has sponsored a project to encourage the reporting of, and dealing with, problems of racial harassment [CASE STUDY 3].

CASE STUDY 3

'Alert' anti-racial harassment agency in London Borough of Newham

Background

The London Borough of Newham had a process in place within the housing department to monitor reports of racial attacks within the borough. There was considerable under-reporting of race attacks and, where attacks were reported, the agencies lacked the expertise to investigate complaints and bring cases before the courts. It was also felt that victims lacked confidence in the local police and were afraid to give evidence in court for fear of reprisal. Members were keen to increase the number of legal actions against perpetrators, and existing measures were considered to be of limited impact.

Action

The council therefore opted to contract out its service for preventing racial harassment. A specialist agency, Estate Management UK Ltd., was asked to run an anti-harassment agency, 'Alert in Newham'. The agency aims to provide:

• an emergency helpline;

• a case investigation service;

• evidence for use in court cases; and

• regular statistics to the council.

Results

Alert had a caseload in excess of 450 cases for 1998. Of those cases, about 20 have a realistic prospect of legal action through the civil courts. Information is now being shared between the police, council and Alert. This close joint working has meant that, in several cases, action in the criminal courts by the police has been complemented by civil action, such as injunctions and possession proceedings. A protocol for exchanging information between the police, council and Alert is now in place.

Alert has also helped victims of racial harassment to be rehoused where the victim was too afraid to take action. Broader inter-agency co-operation is now being sought, using a 'case conference' forum, to ensure that agencies come together and devise the best possible solutions for victims (and deal effectively with perpetrators) of racial harassment.

Good practice points

• the council and police responded to the needs of a group that was not confident about reporting its problems to public agencies; and

• recognising their lack of expertise in-house, the agencies concerned pursued an innovative approach to tackle the problem.

148. In high-crime areas, considerable resources may be needed to ensure that local communities are given confidence to maintain a safe environment. This process is sometimes called 'capacity building' and requires local leadership from residents, agencies and politicians. A major research project on 20 unpopular housing estates found that *intensive localised (housing) management was as important in arresting decline as reinvestment* (Ref. 55). While the involvement of local people was critical to arresting decline, they needed help and support to manage the estate. The key factors for success that were distilled from this study endorse messages about the need for local approaches to involve local people [EXHIBIT 32].

149. Such concerted efforts must be actively managed to ensure that impact is maximised and that the community is left with a sustainable improvement in safety. In the highest-crime areas this will require a concerted effort at multi-agency working, requiring leadership and, at times, challenges to existing ways of working. These factors were brought together with tremendous energy in Sunderland [CASE STUDY 4].

EXHIBIT 32

Key factors for success in local community safety initiatives

The key factors for success all promote local approaches that involve local people.

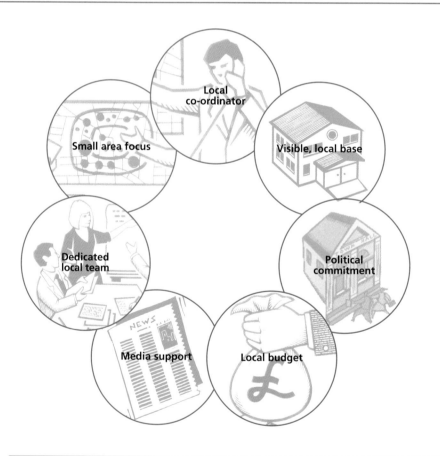

Source: Audit Commission

CASE STUDY 4

Leading locally on community safety in Sunderland

Background

On the Pennywell estate in Sunderland, a regeneration project has been funded by SRB, the City Council and the police over a six-year timescale. The four key strands are:

- community safety;
- employment;
- education; and
- health.

The community safety strand comprises a number of phases, the first of which aims to 'reclaim the estate'. Burglary was 40 times the national average; 43 per cent of all assaults against housing staff in the authority occurred on the estate; and 83 per cent of local residents were concerned by crime 'a lot'. Many victims did not report crime to the police for fear of reprisals from offenders. The Safer Estates Task Force – a project led by the city's health and housing department and the local police division – was set up to focus, in the first instance, on disrupting the activities of offenders, with longer-term work to challenge the prevailing 'culture of crime and drugs' on the estate.

Action

The local police can analyse hotspots, and identify repeat victims and those at risk of victimisation. As a result, they are working with the health and housing department to support new residents by moving them on to the estate in groups and providing enhanced support to those at risk of being victimised.

Although led by housing and police, all agencies on the estate are involved in some way. A residents' association has been developed for the first time, despite a fire attack on the building in which they were due to have their first meeting. This group has taken a lot of nurturing, but has become an essential point of contact for staff. The health and housing department is working very closely with the local school to challenge the prevailing culture and to reward good behaviour. For example, it has a 'junior task force' which has developed its own promotional literature and rules to be part of its club. There is also a breakout scheme, led by the Pennywell Youth project and the Pennywell Neighbourhood Centre, which provides constructive leisure opportunities for young people at risk of offending over school holidays. Other agencies, in particular the voluntary sector and social services, have been very supportive, as have local politicians.

The lead housing officer takes messages back to cross-departmental senior management groups at council level to promote the involvement of mainstream departments. She drew up a report entitled *Suggestions Welcome*, which invited professionals from council departments to visit the estate and take an interest in tackling some of the problems that local residents are experiencing.

Results

- drop in burglary, drop in overall crime levels, reduction of repeat victimisation;
- an unexpected 70 per cent drop in fire brigade attendance during the school holidays, following joint working with Tyne and Wear fire brigade, the junior task force and the local comprehensive school;
- one eviction has taken place, but the majority of cases have been resolved without the need for legal action;
- the number of void properties has stabilised; and
- there has been a 56 per cent reduction year-on-year in the number of people terminating their tenancy. New tenants are staying longer on the estate.

Good practice points

- having the vision to create such an exciting and unique project;
- having an excellent team of staff who believe that they can succeed;
- having a locally based co-ordinator who is also a member of the departmental senior management team, ensuring that issues are raised more generally within the authority; and
- members, local residents and agencies are committed to working together and proving that partnership works.

Reconciling local and national priorities

150. Since a major principle of community safety work is that it should address local concerns, it will be important for partnerships to reconcile local and national priorities. In the short term, this will mean some recognition of a broadening of the agenda and possibly a revised focus on national priorities. Over the longer term, local work has the potential to inform national level decision-making more directly. In order to do this, a national commentary on the progress of partnerships, the problems that they are tackling and of trends over time will be needed. A more general review of the role of national agencies is given in the last section of this chapter.

Developing a learning approach to community safety

There are no 'off-the shelf' solutions to the problems of unsafe communities

151. There are no 'off-the shelf' solutions to the problems of unsafe communities. What is most important is that partnerships learn from their own experiences and from research about what works in particular situations, and appraise critically the different options for strategies appropriate to their areas. In essence, partnerships need to develop a culture of learning.

152. A learning approach to community safety problems goes through the key problem-solving steps, but places significant emphasis on finding out what works locally and feeding back lessons into future strategy development. Thus, particular attention needs to be given to setting up systems that enable partnerships to:

- set baselines for improvement;

- appraise and select the best options for delivering that improvement; and

- monitor processes and outcomes against baselines, learning what works and what does not work.

Setting baselines for improvement

153. Identifying what works requires sound factual knowledge about the problems that partnerships are tackling. In the past this information has not been available – simple questions such as how much disorder exists in an area, and when and where it is concentrated, have not been straightforward to answer.

154. Such baselines must also provide a clear definition and understanding of the problem. Without this, partnerships run the risk of wasting effort, and in effect solving 'the wrong problem'. The police service has had some success in using a problem analysis triangle (PAT) to analyse crime and disorder problems before considering potential solutions (Ref. 56). Information is needed on victims, offenders and locations in order to understand community safety problems and their underlying causes in some detail [EXHIBIT 33].

EXHIBIT 33

Problem analysis triangle

Information is needed on victims, offenders and locations in order to understand community safety problems and their detailed causes.

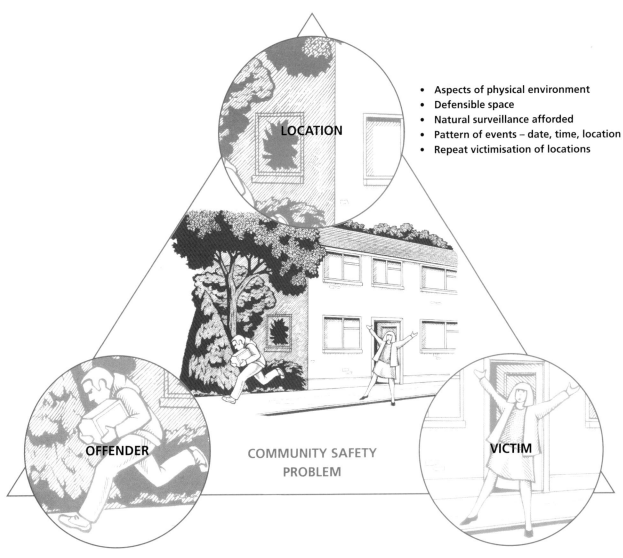

LOCATION

- Aspects of physical environment
- Defensible space
- Natural surveillance afforded
- Pattern of events – date, time, location
- Repeat victimisation of locations

OFFENDER

COMMUNITY SAFETY PROBLEM

VICTIM

- Age, sex, ethnicity
- Risk factors
- Relationship with victim
- Repeat offending

- Age, sex, ethnicity
- Characteristics that make them vulnerable
- Relationship with offender
- Aspects of work or leisure that make them vulnerable
- Repeat victimisation

Source: Cohen and Felson (Ref. 56), Audit Commission analysis

155. To apply the principles of the PAT to community safety, Home Office guidance offers a useful template, bringing together potential information sources on victims, locations and offenders within partner agencies that might inform community safety audits [EXHIBIT 34]. In the first round of audits under the new Crime and Disorder Act, most partnerships will not have been able to review all potential data sources. However, over time it will be important to undertake a broad review of sources, for two reasons:

- partnerships will then be able to understand not only the incidence of community safety problems, but also causes and risk factors. Data on these typically resides in departments with more 'social' functions, such as education and social services. This data will be important for monitoring outcomes; and

- a review will encourage individual partner agencies and departments to invest time and resources in community safety work, since they will be working to a common map that expresses problems in their terms using their data.

EXHIBIT 34

Home Office guidance on audit information sources

There is a wide range of potential information sources within partner agencies that might inform community safety audits.

Source (agency)	Type of data	What it will tell you	What it will NOT tell you
Police force	Crime incidents Offender information Command and control data on non-crime incidents	Time, location, type of offences reported to the police Known offenders by age, gender, ethnicity, address Time, location, type of non-crime offences reported to the police (around 70% of calls)	Levels of reporting vary by crime type Unknown offenders Only covers calls to police
Police authority	Public surveys	Perceptions of safety and fear of crime	Unlikely to be at detailed level
Local authority housing department	Housing voids Criminal damage costs Records of complaints and neighbour disputes Reasons for transfer applications	Costs of crime to housing agencies; likely to cover high crime neighbourhoods Extent of neighbour nuisance and perceptions of quality of life	Costs of crime to private landlords
Local authority social services department	Information on vulnerable groups Information on young offenders	Where to find groups who may be victims of crime or in fear of crime (eg, elderly) Understanding of offender behaviour Complements police data	Concentrates on the most vulnerable known to social services
Local education authority	Exclusions Truancy	Schools where a high percentage of pupils are out of school Risk factor for offending or being victimised Complements police data	Need to establish nature of link between non-attendance and crime locally

EXHIBIT 34 (cont.)

Probation	**Information on offenders**	**Perspective on criminal behaviour and its causes** **Locates known offenders**	Covers only known offenders
Health authority	**Casualty records of assault and domestic violence** **Information on drug-taking**	**Likely to cover offences not reported to police** **Should complement police data on those at risk of offending**	Sources and location of injuries not always recorded Need to establish link between drugs and offending locally
Drug action team	**Information on drug-taking**	**Should complement police and health data**	Likely to have a better understanding of local links between drugs and crime
Fire service	**Incidents of arson; hoax calls and suspicious fires**	**Patterns of incidents** **Complements police data**	Some fires may go unreported Little data on offenders
Community relations council	**Incidents of racial attacks and harassment**	**Patterns of racial crime** **Complements police data**	Only partial reporting

Source: Home Office, Guidance on Statutory Crime and Disorder Partnerships (Ref. 57) – extract

156. Without analysis, collating such data risks becoming an end in itself. For partnerships to compile large databases without understanding their purpose would be a waste of time, effort and money. To be useful, the data must enable agencies to devise a common map of where the problems exist. Audits conducted by fieldwork sites provide simple examples of how data from a number of sources helped to inform their targeting activities and to set useful baselines against which to monitor outcomes [**EXHIBIT 35**].

EXHIBIT 35

Audits that target and set baselines

Audits conducted by fieldwork sites were able to use the data to inform their targeting activities, and set useful baselines against which to monitor outcomes.

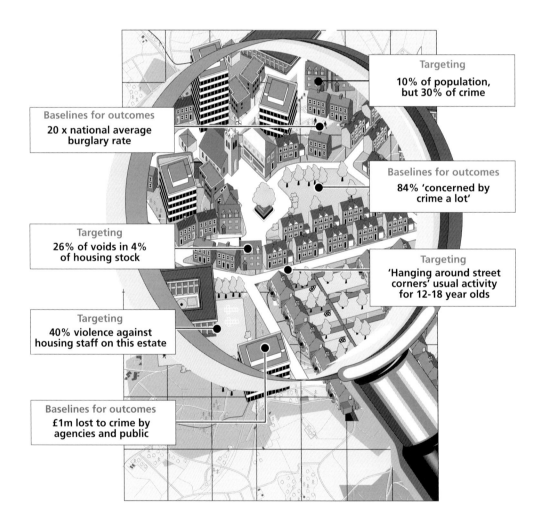

Source: Composite of examples from Audit Commission fieldwork

157. Repeat victimisation is a key indicator that helps partnerships to target their work. Eliminating 'repeats' can be a very efficient means of reducing crime and disorder, and there are several good demonstration projects on burglary schemes (Ref. 58). HMIC found that only half of police forces were able to produce such vital information (Ref. 44). Systems for developing data on 'repeats' will need to be produced if the police contribution to the audit is to be as useful as possible.

158. The first round of audits under the new Act will be a learning experience. Drawing data together to develop a fuller picture will take time and expertise, and will require the development of an information strategy for long-term development [CASE STUDY 5].

CASE STUDY 5

Safer Salford and the Salford Crime Information Strategy

Background

Safer Salford has been in existence since 1989, starting out as a Safer Cities partnership. More recently, it became part of the Safer Salford Partnership to comply with the Crime and Disorder Act. It has been asked to conduct the crime audit and to help to develop the strategy for community safety.

Its expertise in inter-agency work and using data to target its work taught it that crime audits were a very useful tool. However, exercises in the past had been inflexible, expensive and quickly dated. Safer Salford therefore decided to use IT to achieve a more efficient use of information; it has developed a digital-mapping database to compile crime audit information and to enable it to automate the analysis.

The audit and database

Safer Salford is helping to develop a number of community safety area profiles within the borough, in partnership with Greater Manchester Research and Salford University. The database draws data from a number of sources:

- local authority records, including data on risk factors;
- the Census;
- fire service;
- Greater Manchester Police;
- drugs action teams;
- local businesses;
- the health authority;
- probation records;
- 'home watch' schemes; and
- 'perceptions' of crime.

It has formed an audit team of staff from each agency which has produced a matrix, detailing the:

- lead officer for data collection within each department;
- data that they will collect;
- timespan of data;
- breakdown (by street/area/other); and
- frequency of update.

The software package being used enables data from a wide range of sources to be brought together into maps and analysed. The data can be stored by ward, beat, Census enumeration district or any 'user-defined' field.

Results

The database produces local area maps that help to prioritise target areas for further work. The partnership has been successful in using data on repeat burglaries and hoax calls to the fire brigade to direct community safety interventions. The experience has helped to build inter-agency confidence, through forming teams and setting up information-sharing protocols. It has also helped to set quantitative baselines against which to track progress.

Good practice points

- development of an information strategy drawing on previous audits;
- use of data from all partner agencies, including repeat victimisation and risk factors;
- use of quantitative data to set baselines for monitoring and evaluation; and
- use of experts to help to develop the information strategy.

Appraising and selecting options for delivering improvements

159. There is some useful research on 'what works' and 'what's promising' in tackling community safety problems. The Home Office Crime Prevention Agency is currently developing a database of such initiatives through the National Crime Prevention College. Partnerships should learn from evaluations already conducted nationally and internationally on 'what works' [EXHIBIT 36].

160. However, what is less easy to identify is *why a strategy worked and whether it will work as well in another setting*. Partnerships thus need to take a critical approach to appraising the options available and to consider carefully whether the strategy will have an immediate impact or a sustained benefit. The Home Office evaluation of the Safer Cities anti-burglary initiatives illustrates how a critical approach can aid an understanding of why and in what settings a strategy can be most effective [BOX D].

EXHIBIT 36

Examples of evaluations of community safety work

Partnerships should learn from evaluations already conducted nationally and internationally on 'what works'.

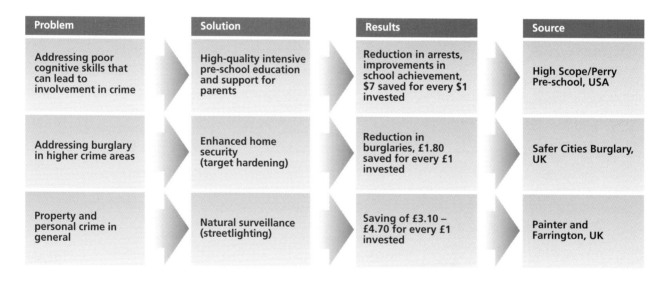

Problem	Solution	Results	Source
Addressing poor cognitive skills that can lead to involvement in crime	High-quality intensive pre-school education and support for parents	Reduction in arrests, improvements in school achievement, $7 saved for every $1 invested	High Scope/Perry Pre-school, USA
Addressing burglary in higher crime areas	Enhanced home security (target hardening)	Reduction in burglaries, £1.80 saved for every £1 invested	Safer Cities Burglary, UK
Property and personal crime in general	Natural surveillance (streetlighting)	Saving of £3.10 – £4.70 for every £1 invested	Painter and Farrington, UK

Source: Home Office, Reducing Offending (Ref. 59)

BOX D

Safer Cities and domestic burglary

A comprehensive cost-benefit analysis of the burglary initiatives within the Safer Cities programme revealed that, overall, the programme yielded savings of £31 million – about the same cost as the programme. However, the cost per burglary prevented was lower in areas that were burgled more intensively (£300 vs £1,100), improving the payoff from investment in higher-crime areas. Physical (or situational) crime prevention measures worked independently, but measures that relied on involving local communities needed reinforcement. However, a combination of both worked better still. Low-intensity crime prevention effort displaced burglary to nearby areas and to other crimes. In order to have an impact on fear of crime, people needed to be aware of action in the area. Intensive action was most likely to affect fear of crime. Moreover, the perception of an area's quality improved where crime prevention action was most intensive.

Source: Safer Cities and Domestic Burglary, Home Office Research Study, 1996 (Ref. 60)

Where partnerships... critically appraise options, they are more likely to select cost-effective strategies

161. However, any initiatives should be tailored to the problem in hand. Having analysed a given community safety problem in more detail, partnerships can begin to work by addressing elements of that problem. Different aspects of burglary problems suggest different modes of intervention [EXHIBIT 37, overleaf].

162. Where partnerships are aware of relevant research and can critically appraise options, they are more likely to select cost-effective strategies and be equipped to respond to public demands for (sometimes expensive) solutions. In one fieldwork site, the community safety co-ordinator put together a report into what was known about the effectiveness of CCTV and therefore how it might best be used, and used it to inform requests by members for investment in CCTV cameras.

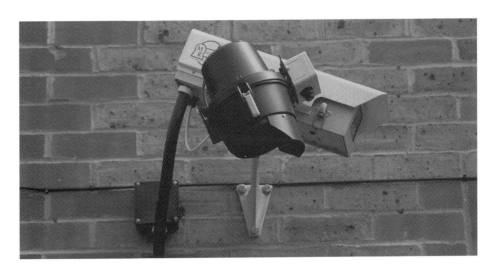

EXHIBIT 37

Solutions to burglary, using the problem analysis triangle (PAT)

Having analysed a given community safety problem in more detail, partnerships can begin to work by addressing specific characteristics of that problem.

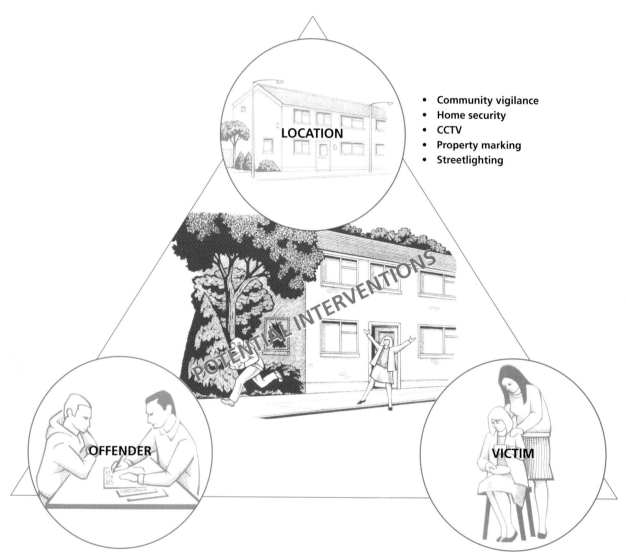

LOCATION

- Community vigilance
- Home security
- CCTV
- Property marking
- Streetlighting

OFFENDER

- Education and control of truancy
- Community development – tackling alcohol and drug abuse
- Identification of offenders and effective police investigation
- Locating stolen goods

VICTIM

- Victim support
- Witness support
- Identification of repeat victims

Source: Audit Commission

Monitoring and learning

163. Having selected a given strategy and set its objectives, the partnership will need to design a mechanism for monitoring outcomes. Performance indicators will be needed to track overall progress as well as that of individual projects. An illustrative performance framework for the overall strategy is contained in Appendix 2 to this report. More detailed information should be tailored to the objective of each project, tracking a number of relevant measures and how these relate to outcomes that affect people's quality of life [BOX E].

BOX E

Monitoring and evaluation of youth disorder

	Example 1	Example 2
Objective	Develop a strategy to reduce the number of reports of disorder occurring outside a community sports facility.	Implement a programme of measures to reduce sporadic outbreaks of youth disorder on a large housing estate.
Process	Collate and analyse all reports, as well as police intelligence records. Profile the incidents, including the characteristics of complainants as well as perpetrators. Diagnose why incidents occur where, and when, they do.	'Understand the problem' from available statistics (as in example 1), but also consult youth service and hold focus groups with community. Profile family and educational background of young people involved. Determine action required.
Input	Initial effort required from police, or researcher, in scoping the problem. Options for intervention then need to be tabled before a group comprising all agencies is likely to be able to assist.	Analysis, leading to agreement about programme of measures. Resources needed to fund interventions: for example, a detached youth worker; support measures for key families and the establishment of improved recreational facilities.
Target outputs	Clear analysis of the nature of the problem and 'players' involved and guidance on how disorder is triggered. Identify preventative options. Involve key agencies in strategy development.	Appoint youth worker and evidence of his/her ability to establish links with local youth. Willingness of families to avail themselves of support. Use made of new recreational facilities.
Target outcomes	Strategy agreed with clear lines of responsibility for all players involved. Resources made available. Monitoring mechanism in place.	Reduction in reports of youth disorder generally, and in particular of those involving young people targeted.

Source: Audit Commission analysis

The Safer Merseyside Partnership has shown imaginative and pragmatic approaches to designing monitoring systems

164. The difficulty in monitoring and evaluating the outcomes of community safety projects should be acknowledged. Monitoring and evaluating the impact of social approaches to promoting community safety can be especially difficult, and often require tracking over the long term. The Safer Merseyside Partnership has shown imaginative and pragmatic approaches to designing monitoring systems that benefit, in particular, from close links with the local university [CASE STUDY 6].

CASE STUDY 6

Safer Merseyside – a learning partnership

Background

The Safer Merseyside Partnership is co-ordinated by the Merseyside Police Authority (MPA) and comprises representatives from all five metropolitan authorities, Merseyside Police, Mersey Transport, the Probation Service, the private and voluntary sectors and the fire authority. The partnership draws on funds from a variety of sources, but is primarily funded by external finance (SRB, EU), having raised in excess of £10 million since 1995.

The MPA, as the accountable body for the work of the partnership, takes responsibility for the administration and financial management of the entire partnership and prepares and submits applications for external funding. It places a strong emphasis on the use of research into 'what works' and monitoring and evaluating new projects, and has imposed this rigour on those seeking access to its funding. Consequently all bids are assessed through a series of local community safety committees and at a borough level for compliance with and contribution to both local and regional community safety plans. The MPA also has an agreement with Liverpool University to analyse information on local crime and disorder issues, making extensive use of geograpical information systems (GIS) to help to determine decisions on further programme development and resource allocation. The University also helps to evaluate new schemes to inform strategy development.

Action and results

One such scheme is the Youth Action Programme – a set of outreach projects with socially excluded teenagers in targeted neighbourhoods throughout Merseyside. It has developed a set of measures for recording the types of contact with young people and is tracking, through user surveys, young people's own assessment of their situation, opportunities and life chances in general. The surveys are providing valuable information to help to improve the targeting of local services to young people's needs.

A second scheme was a study with the local fire brigade of hoax calls. Such calls accounted for 25 per cent of calls to the brigade, wasting millions of pounds. Using GIS, the University plotted the location and timing of calls and identified that 20 per cent of calls came from just 3 per cent of phone boxes.

CASE STUDY 6 (cont.)

The study also found that hoax calls were concentrated between 6 and 8 pm. The police then installed covert surveillance in the top ten phone boxes for hoax calls, as well as conducting an intensive programme of community fire safety education in schools. A similar analytical approach was used to tackle the problem of arson. The work has achieved a 40 per cent reduction in malicious false alarms and a 48 per cent reduction in arson between July 1996 and July 1997.

A third scheme is a study of repeat victimisation of small businesses. Like many urban community safety partnerships, Safer Merseyside is concerned about the vulnerability of such businesses and the impact their failure may have on the economy and safety of the immediate locality. Many businesses in specific areas suffered from multiple burglaries and attempted break-ins, causing some eventually to fail and move out, leaving behind empty property that became difficult to let. Business vulnerability from crime had wider repercussions on the whole community.

The partnership is now focusing on developing links with the prison service, to address the needs of those who have been in prison in an attempt to prevent reoffending.

Good practice points

- the leadership group takes responsibility for programme management and evaluation;

- the local university acts as independent, objective broker, informing rigorous strategies; and

- there is a strong emphasis on monitoring and evaluation, assisted by independent experts from local university, enables partnership to focus on outcomes.

The best partnerships were very aware of the developments in research into what works

165. Bringing together the different strands of a learning approach to community safety requires long-term planning. The best partnerships were very aware of the developments in research into *what works*, and this pool of knowledge should be tapped before opting for strategies that may already have been proven not to be cost-effective. However, attitudes, skills and systems have taken time to develop, and partnerships will need to invest in resources and people to reap the benefits of the learning approach advocated above.

Developing an investment approach to community safety

166. Chapter 2 identified problems with generating investment in community safety as well as accounting for community safety activities. Without resources, strategies cannot be implemented. Without being able to identify resources – whether cash or in kind, such as people's time – partnerships will be unable to account for their activities. In the early stages of this new field, three areas are of particular importance:

- the use of seedcorn budgets to 'build the case' for investing further in community safety;

- developing a pragmatic approach to financial and activity accounting for investments in community safety; and

- investing in people to develop community safety.

Using seedcorn budgets to build commitment

167. Throughout the fieldwork for this study, enthusiasts described how individual projects, which were not in themselves expensive, had made the case for further investment in community safety. For partnerships that are just starting out, pump-priming will be needed to kick start this process. Pump-priming resources, together with the sound analysis and reporting described later in this chapter, can generate a virtuous circle of investment in prevention [**EXHIBIT 38**].

168. Cost-benefit analysis is a useful way of persuading partners and outside investers to invest in prevention. Analysing issues on a smaller scale – focusing the measurement of costs on housing departments, hospitals or schools – can be more directly useful than broad statements of cost across large geographic areas. Quantifying the costs of community safety problems provides a baseline and allows an understanding of potential savings that could be accrued by addressing the problem.

EXHIBIT 38

Pump-priming virtuous circle

Pump-priming resources, together with sound analysis and reporting, can generate a virtuous circle of investment in prevention.

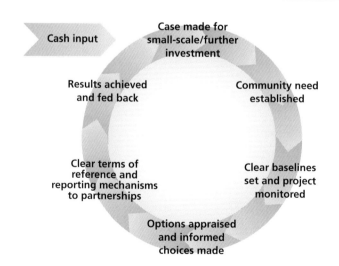

Source: Audit Commission

169. Many councils already do this through their work on 'risk management'; for example, attempting to reduce the exposure of public buildings to maintenance and vandalism costs. The approach – which involves quantifying the level of exposure and investing in reducing it – is a useful model for promoting community safety. The Accounts Commission in Scotland undertook a study of risk management in schools and discovered that more was spent on responding to crime and other risk management issues than was spent on books in 1996/97 (Ref. 28). One authority was able to use such analysis to justify expenditure on graffiti and vandalism [CASE STUDY 7].

CASE STUDY 7

Cost-benefit approach to reducing graffiti and vandalism in Swansea

Background

Swansea City and County Council was concerned at the level of graffiti and other vandalism in the area. Local school headteachers were reporting the high cost of addressing the problems of vandalism and graffiti. The council officers knew from research that fear of crime, resulting from graffiti, rubbish and a general atmosphere of neglect, can lead to an area being stigmatised and, at worst, becoming a 'no go' area. Reducing fear of crime was a priority for the corporate community safety strategy.

Action

The council formed a risk management group in 1995, which produced figures from all departments on the costs to the local authority of vandalism. These totalled over £2 million per year. Further analysis of the problem showed that 90 per cent of the graffiti involved the use of indelible marker pens, and that most offenders were aged 9 to 16. Commercial removal of the graffiti

was quite expensive, and so the council opted for a lower-cost option, purchasing environmentally friendly chemicals and using people on community service orders from the probation service and local pupils to do the work. Consistent removal was found to be effective in eventually reducing vandalism.

Results

Graffiti did not completely disappear, but no serious acts of vandalism were subsequently reported. In parallel, the police liaison officer and the fire safety officer visited local schools in an attempt to deter destructive behaviour. The project has been very popular with all involved, has effectively been a low-cost 'quick win', and has led to further work on vandalism and broader community safety work. For example, since the original project, vandalism to bus shelters has been costed at £56,000 and a further contribution of £2,000 was made by the Highways and Technical Department to tackle this problem. A local school has won a national

award for its work in setting pupils to take a more responsible attitude to school buildings.

Good practice points

- putting a cost on vandalism created a case for action; through research, the council was also aware of the broader impact of the problem;

- the interdepartmental risk management group surveyed costs across the authority;

- the search for a low-cost response ensured that savings were made;

- the use of environmentally friendly chemicals meant that pupils could be involved and enjoy addressing destructive behaviour; and

- a successful cost-benefit approach led to further investment by other council departments.

Partnerships are recognising the need to account for activities that contribute to community safety

170. Central government can play a useful role in encouraging partnerships by targeting challenge funding or the £250 million in the new Crime Reduction Strategy to invest in what works and in appropriate opportunities to learn and evaluate. Too great an emphasis on 'national solutions' is to miss opportunities to tailor solutions effectively to local problems, and acts as a disincentive for partnerships to develop learning approaches.

Financial and activity accounting for community safety

171. A general problem with quantifying investment concerns the capturing of activity in mainstream service departments that is budgeted under different headings. However, a cost-benefit analysis cannot be attempted without an understanding of the costs of activities. Increasingly, partnerships are recognising the need to account for activities that contribute to community safety where they are material [**CASE STUDY 8**].

CASE STUDY 8

Accounting for community safety expenditure in Epsom and Ewell

Background

Epsom and Ewell Borough Council has a separate cost centre for community safety. However, in calculating the full cost of initiatives, the community safety officer identified that the costs of community safety activities were accounted for under a variety of headings and that 'hidden' costs were sometimes incurred by departments.

For example, the co-ordination and planning of multi-agency public events, where the full costs were shared between departments and organisations, were detailed under different headings. Even the preparation on a basic publicity leaflet requires time and costs from a range of people, from the originator to publicity and printing.

Action

The co-ordinator worked first with different departments within the borough to identify all the different sources of expenditure on community safety. This exercise found, for example, that:

- maintenance, monitoring and running costs of CCTV came under separate headings;

- staff costs, photocopying, postage and leaflets came under various central services headings;

- community safety grants were accounted for separately; and

- contributions from other agencies – such as the police and county council – were accounted for in different income codes.

CASE STUDY 8 (cont.)

Much community safety expenditure is now coded separately so that the council can easily track resources committed to community safety activities. The community safety officer also records the time spent on different initiatives to ensure that use of her time is recognised.

Results

The exercise has proved useful in identifying the full costs of activities, bringing together a fragmented picture across the organisation. For example, detailed costs of putting on an event are now known. Informed decisions about resource allocation can now be made within multi-agency partnership meetings, rather than by staff within separate agencies who might see only part of the picture.

Good practice points

- identification of contributions to community safety within each agency;

- identification of the full costs of activities, including the time of key staff, allowing realistic planning;

- coding of key expenditure to ensure that it can be tracked under a community safety heading; and

- work with the finance department to change and refine systems to ensure this can be done in the future.

The ideal financial reporting format should reflect the aims and objectives of the partnership

172. The ideal financial reporting format should reflect the aims and objectives of the partnership. This should include a statement of where resource contributions come from and what they are then invested in – a joint investment plan. Safer Merthyr Tydfil Partnership has already adopted this form of financial reporting [CASE STUDY 9, overleaf]. In practice, this approach will not be possible for the majority of mainstream activities, since they will already be budgeted through mainstream budgets. However, as described above, some finance departments have started to customise their systems to record community safety expenditure separately once it has been identified as a high priority to do so.

SMT has found that it has been able to make the case for further investment by demonstrating the cost-effective use of existing resources

CASE STUDY 9

Safer Merthyr Tydfil's financial systems and reporting

Background

Safer Merthyr Tydfil (SMT) has operated since 1995, handling increasingly large amounts of expenditure and securing grants from different sources. Since it is accountable to a number of organisations, clear and sound financial management is essential to its work.

Action

SMT has a management team that includes an office manager who tracks European finance, which forms the greatest part of SMT's income. A finance manager is responsible for day-to-day book-keeping and financial management. The annual report clearly identifies sources and uses of funds, so that expenditure priorities can be traced.

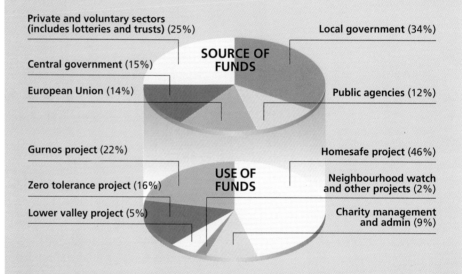

Private and voluntary sectors (includes lotteries and trusts) (25%)

Central government (15%)

European Union (14%)

SOURCE OF FUNDS

Local government (34%)

Public agencies (12%)

Gurnos project (22%)

Zero tolerance project (16%)

Lower valley project (5%)

USE OF FUNDS

Homesafe project (46%)

Neighbourhood watch and other projects (2%)

Charity management and admin (9%)

Results

SMT has found that, over time, it has been able to make the case for further investment by demonstrating the cost-effective use of existing resources. For example, the majority of expenditure is on the 'Homesafe' service (see also Case Study 12), which secures the homes of vulnerable residents at a cost of £70 per household. This expenditure can be offset by the estimated cost of responding to a burglary (approximately £1,150 for each victim, 16 hours of police time and £44 for the emergency call-out fee for the local authority housing department).

Good practice points

*   having staff in place to collate and analyse budget information;
*   clear financial reporting, outlining the source and use of funds; and
*   cost-benefit approach, making the case for further investment.

Source: Safer Merthyr Tydfil, Annual Report, 1997/98

Those at senior levels within partner agencies must own the issue of community safety

Investing in people for community safety

173. Chapter 2 highlighted the lack of available people and skills to do much of the new work required for community safety. There is no simple 'fix' for this problem, and its solution must be managed at a number of levels and will take time to implement. Appropriate people need to be developed in three areas:

- top managers to 'champion' and lead on community safety;

- technicians who can develop the practice of community safety; and

- local managers who can work to engage local communities and develop capacity where needed.

174. Those at senior levels within partner agencies must own the issue of community safety before many of the changes outlined in this report can begin to take hold. This is not simply a matter of informing people and building awareness, but involves signalling community safety as a priority through the full range of human resource management mechanisms, from recruitment through to appraisal, training, promotion and career development [CASE STUDIES 10 and 11].

CASE STUDIES

Signalling the importance of community safety to top managers: Basildon and West Yorkshire Police

CASE STUDY 10

Basildon Top Management Programme

Basildon District Council has established a multi-agency partnership made up of senior representatives of the public, private and voluntary sectors. Meetings of the Better Basildon Partnership enable participants to discuss and agree a multi-agency response to problems identified within the district. Community safety and the links with other strategic initiatives have been a regular item on the partnership's agenda.

In response to the Government's agenda, the partnership has agreed the need for a multi-agency regeneration plan and has funded a training programme to help the partnership to develop and implement the plan. The training programme has been designed by the partnership with the support of the Office for Public Management which will be providing the training. Community safety, youth development, healthy living, education and job creation are themes that the partnership intends the regeneration plan to address.

Basildon District Council has also developed a Top Managers Training Programme for senior officers of the council, and with some participation from local police officers. The programme is based on a set of managerial and leadership competencies, which have been developed in partnership with the Office for Public Management, the programme's appointed consultants.

continued overleaf

CASE STUDY 10 (cont.)

The purpose of the programme is to equip Basildon's senior managers with the skills that are needed to meet current and future challenges, to foster a greater understanding of partnership working and to encourage officers to work across service boundaries. Crime reduction and community safety is one area in which the programme is already facilitating change.

CASE STUDY 11

West Yorkshire Police promotion boards

West Yorkshire Police has signalled to career-minded police officers that community safety is a top priority by making it a topic for discussion at promotion boards. Since this approach was adopted, the community safety co-ordinator has had numerous contacts from officers wanting to know more about community safety.

Good practice points (both case studies)

- putting community safety on the map by using human resource mechanisms such as training or promotion boards.

175. In all agencies, a greater appreciation is needed of the practice of community safety. In common with other preventative disciplines, community safety suffers from a lack of professional status (Ref. 46). The Home Office and Local Governnment Association (LGA) are pursuing a national training strategy and forthcoming Home Office guidance will help to inform this process. This work is vitally important to ensure that community safety is informed and that the knowledge base of 'what works' is kept up-to-date. Local government officers have already formed a national network both in England and in Wales, and this needs to be properly supported and developed.

176. Finally, dynamic local managers are needed who can engage communities that are hard to reach and which need support. Such skills already exist in some agencies, such as education welfare, youth work and social work, but need to be developed in a more concerted way, either by a lead agency or by all agencies. Community safety work will not be effective if the right people are not made available.

177. In this new field, there is much for agencies to achieve in developing appropriate financial and human resources. Without these resources, partnerships cannot be sure of delivering community safety, since they will not be able to identify activities or find people to make them successful.

Developing accountable and delivery-focused partnerships

178. An effective partnership organisation is needed, not only to build an effective strategy, but also to ensure effective delivery of that strategy. The previous chapter described how holding partnerships to account is particularly difficult, since their activities are complex and often hidden. Of particular importance therefore are the systems, processes and protocols that enable partnerships to have clarity of objectives and to operate smoothly.

Establishing a common vision and roles

179. Given the very different organisational styles and backgrounds of partnership staff, establishing a common vision of what the partnership aims to achieve as well as an understanding of the roles within it is vital. It should not be assumed that this will happen automatically. Partnerships need to establish their vision of a healthy community and a 'constitution' for how they intend to achieve it [CASE STUDY 12].

CASE STUDY 12

Safer Merthyr Tydfil's mission statement and constitution

Background

The Safer Merthyr Tydfil Partnership (SMT) was set up in 1995 and forms part of a wider attempt to regenerate the Merthyr Tydfil area. Its mission statement is:

To enhance the quality of life of residents, visitors and those who work or invest in Merthyr Tydfil by reducing crime and fear of crime.

The partnership is managed and guided by a board of trustees and advisers from a number of different agencies. Annual reports are produced that outline budgets and report on targets achieved.

Action

The key strands to the strategy are:

- a 'Homesafe' burglary project, which focuses on securing homes of those vulnerable to burglary;

- reduction in fear of crime, through neighbourhood watch and 'zero tolerance' approaches and area regeneration strategies; and

- grant aid to resident support organisations.

Results

The partnership has placed a strong emphasis on monitoring and evaluating projects, with a view to spreading successful initiatives. In particular, its 'Homesafe' project has been extremely successful in eliminating repeat burglary, reducing burglary by 69 per cent and fear of crime by 50 per cent since its inception. That tangible success has enabled the partnership to convince others to join and invest further in its work (particularly longer-term schemes to reduce offending behaviour, such as

work with socially excluded teenagers). Funding has gone from strength to strength and SMT is now in a position to have a sound management structure and communicate to other partnerships what it has learned.

Good practice points

- clear statements of intent in mission statement;

- clear links between projects and managing board;

- public documents outlining targets and performance; and

- building upon visible success to strengthen the partnership and broaden its activities.

Developing partnership infrastructure

180. To enable partnerships to run smoothly, some infrastructure of people and systems is required. Currently, many agencies have just one member of staff working full-time on community safety but, in practice, links need to be established between the partner agencies at a number of levels. Some fieldwork sites were beginning to develop these links through a mixture of secondments and appointments within the organisation [CASE STUDY 13].

CASE STUDY 13

Partnership links at different levels of the organisation in Basildon

Background

In Basildon, the police and local authority have a history of working closely together on community safety issues. In 1997, the newly-appointed police commander realised that existing police structures and deployment could be realigned to improve partnership working with the local authority and with other agencies and to direct police resources more effectively to areas of greatest need.

Action

Basildon Police decided to develop its own community safety department, which works closely with Basildon District Council. Special efforts have been made to improve joint working opportunities by:

- appointing a community safety sergeant, who co-ordinates all crime reduction work undertaken by Basildon police in partnership with other agencies;

- providing open-plan office space at the police station in order to encourage partner agencies to work with the police;

- harmonising staffing structures between the police community safety department and the local authority community regeneration unit. The community safety sergeant works closely with local authority counterparts;

- using joint police/council forums to consult with the public;

- developing community policing by decentralising officers, moving them to section stations and thereby promoting closer contact with the community; and

- adopting a problem-orientated, as opposed to a reactive, policing style.

The divisional commander is committed to multi-agency crime reduction and works closely with the local authority chief executive.

Results

Through these structures and approaches it is possible for the police to work more closely with the local authority to ensure that their work is best targeted to promote community safety. For example:

- *Basildon Autocrime Strategy Group* – multi-agency collaboration between police, council and local businesses to reduce car crime;

- *Bonus Scheme* – staff from Basildon police, Basildon District Council and local businesses act as volunteer mentors for young people who are least likely to find employment on leaving school

- *Essex Experience/Basildon Challenge* – summer activity camp to promote self-esteem in young people from Basildon district. Camps are staffed by volunteers from police, council and Scouts.

Good practice points

- identification of key roles and joint work to bridge interfaces at different levels of each partner organisation;

- creation of posts for analysis and policy work; and

- joint leadership between local police and local authority.

Given the complexity of partnership operations, it is essential that expectations and accountabilities are clear

181. Such teams need to work out the implications of joint working between agencies. In particular, they have to address issues of information-sharing and communicating between agencies. Dyfed Powys police force was taking the initiative in developing information-sharing protocols with its local authorities to ensure that the Crime and Disorder audit was compiled as smoothly as possible.

Reporting on delivery

182. Many existing strategy documents do not provide a clear audit trail. Given the complexity of partnership operations, it is essential that expectations and accountabilities are clear. Some of the best links between partnerships and local delivery were seen in SRB projects, where it is a requirement of funding that accountability systems are set up with named accountable managers and links made to departmental plans. The Merton strategy pulls this together through a system of targets, lead agencies and deadlines [CASE STUDY 14].

CASE STUDY 14

London Borough of Merton Partnership – Community Safety Strategy

Background

Merton Community Safety partnership has been operating for some years, and has used its experience in community safety regeneration work and joint working to produce an area-wide strategy document, outlining targets and accountabilities among the partners that can be measured and monitored.

Action

The strategy contains four over-arching strategic objectives:

- to support the community to reduce crime and the fear of crime;
- to tackle the causes of crime;

- to tackle specific crime problems; and
- to reduce crime opportunities.

In relation to these objectives, there are a number of strategic targets (across the area, such as racial assault) and specific targets (such as youth crime and particular neighbourhoods), which have been identified by the borough-wide audit. Each of these targets is covered in an action plan. Each action plan identifies the following:

- aim/target;
- lead agency;
- baseline;
- objectives, with outcomes and performance measures; and
- deadline.

In some cases, the performance measures are not actually outcome targets, but represent more intermediate stages – such as setting up a group or reporting on a problem. Nonetheless, each target is designed to be measurable or capable of being monitored and reported back to the strategic group.

Good practice points

- lead agency designations ensure accountability; and
- partnership has a manageable set of priorities and a clear system for tracking performance and holding initiatives to account.

183. Beyond this, individual projects need their own terms of reference, action plans and reporting procedures. For example, Epping Forest District Council has produced a standard template terms of reference for local projects to work to which identifies:

- aims and objectives;

- timescale and resources;

- performance information; and

- reporting mechanisms and review dates.

Integrating community safety into the mainstream

184. Community safety should be an acknowledged responsibility of the police, YOTs, local authority departments and other partners. As the importance of community safety underpinned by the new Act sinks in, partners will need to change their priorities and processes to achieve community safety outcomes – for example, education of those at risk, targeted youth work, or targeted grants to voluntary organisations.

185. Section 17 of the Crime and Disorder Act requires all partner agencies to review the community safety implications of their work. This assessment must be prioritised and worked through carefully to be effective. The key to making this happen is to generate awareness and ownership of community safety so that mainstream agencies see it as part of their work. There are a number of levels at which awareness and ownership need to take root:

- among staff within local partnerships;

- aligning departmental planning within local partnerships;

- aligning corporate processes within local partnerships; and

- ensuring a coherent framework for services at the national level.

Generating awareness and ownership

Deciding which community safety problems to address requires an appreciation of 'what's in it' for each of the partners

186. Staff within different agencies and departments may or may not understand how their work relates to community safety or even see why they should contribute to addressing any problems. To be successful, partnerships must overcome these obstacles. The results of the audit should enable them to identify common problems. Deciding which community safety problems to address requires an appreciation of *what's in it* for each of the partners. In one authority, the housing manager used arguments of cost to convince the local school to work with her to combat crime and anti-social behaviour generally. The school was losing 19 pupils per year from parents wishing to transfer off the estate and had problems with truancy and exclusions. Some innovative approaches to encouraging such shared objectives were found in fieldwork sites [CASE STUDY 15].

CASE STUDY 15

Encouraging partnership development: the Safer Surrey Partnership

Background

The Safer Surrey Partnership Team was launched in October 1992, in response to the Morgan report. It acts as a catalyst, providing a range of services to encourage and promote partnership working across Surrey to achieve safer communities.

Action

The Safer Surrey Partnership enjoys a pooled budget in 1998/99 of £407,800 from the police and county. Team members are seconded from police, probation, education, social services and the fire and rescue services. This enables each agency to derive more than the benefit of its own contribution alone and, at times, to enable 'critical mass' for funding concerted efforts. The secondments encourage exchange of data and ideas and the team is able to provide support to the voluntary sector and new projects.

Results

Specific examples include work with young offenders on a motor project – without partnership funding, this would not have been possible, because no single agency had the budget to undertake this project. The team also set up the Surrey Travellers Community Relations Forum, the first of its kind in the country. Its work aims to harmonise relationships between the travelling and wider communities in the county by bringing together gypsies, travellers, members of the circus community and showmen's guild with public agencies. Furthermore, the partnership has been able to support a network of local mediation services, and to support them in developing a more professional approach to managing their service.

Good practice points

- the work of Safer Surrey ensures that mainstream agencies begin to see 'what's in it for them' to contribute to community safety work; and

- the use of secondments has developed agency awareness.

Implications for mainstream services

187. Much activity in mainstream departments within fieldwork sites could easily have been claimed to be promoting community safety. However, promoting community safety must not simply be an exercise in 're-branding' but should involve targeting work towards tangible community safety outcomes wherever possible. Some sites had started to 'audit' the mainstream services as a first step to promoting a corporate approach to community safety. For example, one former Safer Cities partnership appointed a police officer to interview local authority staff and identify information sources and current initiatives within the council that might be of relevance to community safety. Bradford Council has attempted to address community safety corporately in its best value pilot, which is on community safety [CASE STUDY 16].

CASE STUDY 16

City of Bradford Metropolitan District Council's corporate approach to community safety

Background

In common with many organisations, Bradford Council has been structured on a functional basis, which has not been conducive to a corporate approach to cross-departmental issues such as community safety. In an attempt to adopt a more corporate approach while fulfilling traditional service requirements, it has implemented a new planning process.

Action

Bradford identified five corporate priorities:

1. *Rebuilding communities* – making sure that the whole community contributes to, and benefits from, citizenship of the Bradford Metropolitan District;

2. *Partnerships for local regeneration* – forging partnerships to bring about integrated and sustainable economic, social, health and environmental regeneration for everyone;

3. *Better education for all* – action to improve educational standards and create a world-class workforce;

4. *A clean, healthy and valued environment* – district-wide action to tackle the environmental problems that affect health and quality of life; and

5. *Fighting crime for a safer district* – fighting crime, fear of crime and the causes of crime.

The political and senior management structures were changed to reflect these priorities, and a community plan (1997-2000) was developed to implement the priorities. The fifth priority was successfully put forward as a bid for a best value pilot. One of the requirements of best value is that all services should be reviewed over five years; dividing up priorities in this way will enable Bradford to review all services within this timeframe.

The best value bid outlined the key directorates and services, and the contribution that they could make to achieving positive community safety outcomes.

Results

Performance indicators (PIs) and targets were drawn up for each service and costing attempted to quantify inputs for key service areas. Strategic PIs have included consultation, analysis of effective partnerships, and reduction in crime and the fear of crime.

Good practice points

- review of key services to identify contributions to community safety outcomes;

- corporate approach to key priorities;

- use of performance management to underpin these priorities; and

- realignment of structure where necessary to make priorities more achievable.

Bradford's corporate approach to community safety

Directorate	Service	Contribution
Social services	• Home care	• Offer safety advice and assistance to 5000 vulnerable residents
	• Youth justice	• Process cases quickly; aim to reduce reoffending
Education	• Exclusion service	• Make provision for excluded pupils
	• School security	• Promote schools work on reducing vandalism, theft and arson
Community and environmental services	• Transportation, planning and design	• Provide CCTV, street lighting, design measures to reduce crime and fear of crime
	• Youth and community	• Provide diversionary activities for young people
Housing and environmental protection	• Tenant development	• Assist development of local groups
	• Tenancy enforcement	• Reduce anti-social behaviour
	• Community mediation	• Resolve neighbour conflict early
	• Safe at home	• Work with police to prevent repeat victimisation

CASE STUDY 17

Surrey Police's mainstream approach to community safety

Background

Surrey Police, some years ago, adopted a geographic model of policing for all its officers to address the community's desire for a truly active local police presence. This model created ownership of a specific area for each individual constable and ownership of a collection of such areas for an area inspector, supported by a number of sergeants. Through this model the Force encouraged the development of a problem-solving approach to local issues focused on the prevention of crime and conflict.

Action

Surrey Police, through the Surrey Police model, have engaged with the local community and partnerships have been developed. The area inspector is identifiable and accountable to the local community and, with the local officer and community representatives, pursues problem solving in the area. This has encouraged community involvement in policing issues and, in conjunction with the Safer Surrey Partnership Team, a number of volunteer schemes have developed. Of particular note are a Force-wide network of mediation schemes aimed at addressing neighbour disputes; the recruiting of a number of parish special constables and the establishment of numerous watch schemes.

Results

Crime has reduced in the Force area year-on-year for five successive years. While it would be inappropriate to attribute such a reduction to a single factor, the involvement of the community in local policing has undoubtedly been significant.

Good practice points

- policing with the community is seen as mainstream policing;
- there is joint ownership of problems and solutions by individual officers and the community;
- solutions are funded through partnership.

188. Other approaches include changing the way services are organised and their style of operation to allow for a more problem-solving, preventative approach to community safety [CASE STUDY 17].

189. Of particular importance will be a review of the links between community safety, work on youth justice and that of drugs (and alcohol) action teams. These three areas are so closely linked that, in many partnerships explicit co-ordination between their separate agendas is being sought. Local partnerships are only now experimenting with ways of how this can be best achieved. Co-ordination is easier where the partnership boundaries are coterminous. In London, two different models have been developed:

- in one London borough, coterminous boundaries between the three groups make it easier to co-ordinate the three agendas. The community safety co-ordinator is being proposed as the natural role to co-ordinate the three agendas, while recognising the different reporting lines of the different groups to different chairs and to central government; and

To enable departments to embrace community safety considerations, corporate planning processes between partners need to be aligned

- in another London borough, an 'inter-agency day' is held regularly at which all the multi-agency forums can meet, allowing agencies to discuss their various inter-agency commitments.

Aligning corporate processes

190. To enable departments to embrace community safety considerations, corporate planning processes between partners need to be aligned. The main processes are as follows:

- formulating the annual policing plan for police forces; and
- core corporate planning processes and forums within local government, including committee processes (such as policy and resources) and any corporate strategies.

191. The annual policing plan will need to take account of the local community safety strategies. Since the plan is the responsibility of the police authority, police authorities will need to be aware of community safety implications and have agreed how to accommodate them into their policing plans.

192. Under current arrangements, local authorities may or may not have a committee structure that allows for community safety implications to be reviewed. Some fieldwork sites were beginning to find ways of introducing corporate priorities on to the agenda through alternative committee structures. For example, many councils are developing a matrix of committees, which allows consideration of traditional services as well as those that cut across departments.

193. Local authorities will in future have to produce a local performance plan (LPP) under the new duty of best value. The development of the LPP will be an ideal opportunity to review contributions by departments to cross-cutting objectives.

Of critical importance will be central government's ability to continue to support change

Ensuring a coherent framework for services at the national level

194. While the Crime and Disorder Act provides a valuable impetus to community safety work, it does not in itself represent a sufficient contribution from central government. It needs to be followed up relentlessly. Much work is already underway within government, but of critical importance will be central government's ability to continue to support change on the following fronts:

- ensuring that a 'corporate' approach is taken to cross-departmental issues within central government;
- promoting a focus on local citizen concerns, rather than top-down universal strategies; and
- providing support for local partnerships to learn and grow.

195. Experiences in other countries could provide useful lessons at this point. Many other countries have developed national strategies for elements of community safety [EXHIBIT 39].

196. The most developed countries in this field, such as New Zealand and the Netherlands, are moving increasingly into the most difficult areas, such as reallocating resources across government and drawing up national strategies, where appropriate, on issues of national concern. In New Zealand, a national strategy for addressing family violence has proven successful in raising awareness and changing attitudes [CASE STUDY 18].

EXHIBIT 39

Role of central government in community safety around the world

Other countries have developed national strategies for elements of community safety.

Country	Agency	Policy		Tools						Resources	
		Plan	Influence	Analysis	What works?	Evaluation	Training	Standards	Citizen support	Given locally	Redistribution
Australia	National Campaign Against Violence and Crime	✓	X	✓	✓	✓	✓	Na	✓	✓	X
Belgium	Permanent Secretary for Prevention Policy	✓	X	X	✓	X	✓	X	✓	✓	X
Canada	National Crime Prevention Centre	✓	✓	X	✓	✓	X	Na	✓	✓	X
France	Delegation Interministerielle a la Ville	✓	✓	X	✓	X	✓	✓	X	✓	X
Netherlands	Crime Prevention Secretariat	✓	✓	✓	✓	✓	✓	✓	✓	✓	✓
New Zealand	Crime Prevention Unit	✓	✓	✓	Na	✓	✓	✓	✓	✓	✓
Sweden	National Crime Prevention Council	Na	✓	✓	Na	✓	X	✓	✓	✓	X
USA	Office of Juvenile Justice and Delinquency Prevention	✓	✓	✓	✓	✓	✓	✓	X	✓	X

Source: International Centre for the Prevention of Crime (ICPC)

The New Zealand national strategy on family violence

Background

In 1993, New Zealand was experiencing a rising tide of violence and increasing public concern about this issue. Research suggested that 80 per cent of violence occurred in the home, mainly perpetrated by men against women. Family violence was therefore seen as the root of violence within the community.

The policy of the national police had been to attempt to mediate when called out to domestic disputes, but research showed that this was not working.

Action

A five-year national strategy was developed by the police in 1993 with the following objectives:

- to encourage reporting of family violence; and
- to deter offenders.

The strategy aimed to do this by raising awareness through awards and publicity campaigns, including commercials and a national helpline. In addition, the police took a harder line of intervening and arresting offenders on the spot, rather than trying to mediate.

Partner agencies in central government were encouraged by the police to participate, using a five-week roadshow to market the strategy to key groups. The police identified a central crime reduction agency to act as sponsor for the project, and worked hard at encouraging the voluntary sector and 'social' departments within government to work together on the project. This work culminated in joint guidelines being issued in 1996 by the Department of Social Welfare, which set out key principles, including a preventative approach and consistency and co-ordination between agencies.

Results

The publicity campaign, which emphasised that family violence is a crime, not just 'a domestic matter', won a number of awards, achieving very high advertising recall.

Reporting increased by 44 per cent in the first year, and there was a 50 per cent increase in self-referrals by men to 'Men for Non-violence' – a voluntary scheme for offenders. The number of women murdered by their partners also fell. There were other unexpected spin-offs, such as a significant drop in armed offender call-outs.

Good practice points

- sound problem identification and desire to change;
- recognition for the need for ownership and leadership of problem;
- persistent engagement with 'renegade' departments;
- the use of national publicity campaign; and
- national guidelines supporting a co-ordinated approach between agencies.

197. In order to achieve this sort of a national strategy, a co-ordinated approach is needed within Whitehall. The recent paper from the Social Exclusion Unit (Ref. 16) proposed cross-departmental task force teams to established the foundations for such work, but this initiative will take time to unfold. The Welsh Office, by virtue of having all of its departments located together, has achieved a more integrated approach to developing policy on issues that cut across departments [**CASE STUDY 19**].

CASE STUDY 19

Integrated policies in Wales

Background

The Welsh Office has a history of trying to work across departments since they are all located under one minister. Recent work aimed at a health agenda has tried to look more broadly at partnerships across the public sector.

Action

In the recent Green Paper – *Better Health, Better Wales* (May 1998) – the Welsh Office has explicitly identified the links between different policy areas and sought local agencies' feedback on how the policy might be developed. Under the chapter, 'Sustainable Health and Well-Being', the Welsh Office set out a number of linked initiatives and sought feedback on how they might be integrated:

- healthy workplaces;
- community safety;
- personal and family support; and
- social exclusion.

In particular, it identified the link between crime and ill-health, referring, for example, to fear of crime leading to anxiety and ill-health.

Good practice points

- a holistic approach to policy formulation by central government; and
- partnership with local agencies in developing the policy agenda.

EXHIBIT 40

Community safety – problems and causes and solutions

This chapter has identified solutions to the key problems outlined in Chapter 2, calling for more systematic management and learning from those involved.

Problems	Causes	Solutions *(case study)*
Poor grounding in local people's views 	• Failure to give sufficient weight to local views • Failure to develop an overall communications strategy • Difficulty in reconciling bottom-up and top-down views	• Develop communications strategy *(1, 2)* • Ensure that groups in high crime areas are supported *(3,4)* • National and local agencies to recognise and work at reconciling tensions *(19)*
Poor grasp of causes of and solutions to community safety problems	• Insufficiently thorough mapping and analysis of problems • Lack of understanding of 'what works' • Insufficient monitoring and evaluation	• Ensure that audits produce an information strategy to develop a fuller picture, including data on repeat victimisation and risk factors *(5)*  • Ensure that partnerships are aware of research, locally and nationally *(6)* • Develop capacity to learn from outcomes of work *(6)*
Under-investment in prevention	• Reliance on external funding • Difficulty in identifying spending on community safety • Under-investment in people	• Develop cost-benefit thinking using pump-priming funds *(7, 9)* • Develop joint investment plans, reviewing departmental contributions *(8, 9)* • Ensure that top managers see community safety as a priority *(10, 11)* • Develop problem-solving skills *(6, 17)*
Unclear rationale for partnership 	• Difficulty in establishing clear ownership and accountability • Complex reporting links to delivery	• Establish common vision and constitution *(12)* • Develop organisational and management infrastructure *(13)* • Develop reporting and accountability mechanisms *(14, 16)*
Lack of integration of community safety with mainstream agencies 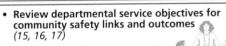	• Mainstream agencies and departments do not see relevance to their work • Crowded corporate agendas • Emphasis on situational project approaches bypassing mainstream departments	• Review departmental service objectives for community safety links and outcomes *(15, 16, 17)* • Encourage multi-agency working on the ground in high crime areas *(2, 4)* • Encourage education and social services departments and health authorities to play full role; promote social approaches to community safety *(16, 18, 19)*

Source: Audit Commission

Conclusion

198. Making a real difference to local communities will require a long-term approach and a step-change in performance from the agencies involved. This chapter has identified solutions to the key problems that were outlined in Chapter 2, calling for more systematic management and learning from those involved.

199. Local agencies have identified an important role for central government in assisting with and supporting change. Many of these roles are being developed centrally, and the success of this work will make a difference to local agencies' ability to learn and grow in this new field of practice on a multi-agency basis.

200. New policies and schemes are being announced by government, many of which impinge on community safety either directly or indirectly. Effective local co-ordination of these separate projects will depend largely on government having a co-ordinated vision of how these initiatives should interact.

Starting to get it right...?

The housing officer said that the council was just starting to work with the police to improve safety on the estate...

She contacted the local councillor who was very keen to be involved and knew a lot of local voluntary organisations. The local police were also very supportive and offered to allocate a community police officer to spend time at the local school to help to educate the children about bullying. The school is also trialling a pupil referral scheme for a while to provide support for excluded children and plan to evaluate its impact. The local headteacher is delighted with this approach.

The officer held a meeting in the local pub. She said that she could not promise miracles, but would work with people on their terms. Some residents made simple suggestions that would make the world of difference, such as ensuring that elderly people were given crime prevention advice and placing streetlighting in notorious dark alley-ways. They're thinking of applying for some grants to build a new community centre.

The housing office has now been located back on the estate and staff have started to get to know the local children by name. The department has started to record the costs of damage as a result of crime on the estate as a way of concentrating the minds of budget-holders back at the local council and are preparing a report for the policy committee.

4

Conclusion and Way Forward

Community safety is a key concern for the general public. Statutory agencies have already started to work together to promote community safety, but effective partnership working will take time to develop and results will not be immediate. Short- and medium-term actions should be taken by local and central government to continue to develop this important work.

The changes that are needed to make the most effective use of public money will take time to unfold

201. Community safety is key to people's quality of life. However, it is an 'outcome' rather than a service. In the past, statutory agencies have ploughed a narrow furrow in concentrating on crime. Consequently, many of the things that make people feel unsafe were accorded a lower priority and the agencies involved failed to achieve a real citizen focus.

202. Many – though not all – have recognised this problem. Central government has made a number of challenge funds available to partnerships, and local agencies have taken considerable initiative and achieved much already. However, much of this activity has been unco-ordinated and of limited demonstrable impact. Until now, no statutory agency has really owned this problem. Yet there is much that can be done, looking across services, to deal with safety problems and their causes, with a view to containing, reducing or preventing them from happening in the first place.

203. The new Crime and Disorder Act provides a major impetus to improve the co-ordination and focus of existing efforts, but partnerships will have to pay particular attention to the management of this major change to achieve the full benefit for local communities. A narrow 'compliance' approach to the Crime and Disorder Act will not meet the scale of the challenge of achieving a real citizen focus.

204. This report has aimed to identify the main problems encountered to date by work on promoting community safety. Many such programmes have failed to achieve the citizen focus that they aimed to champion. Few showed a thorough understanding of local problems, their causes and what might work in addressing them. Work has invariably lacked a clear investment plan, identifying cash and human resources. Partnerships themselves have been unclear about their purpose or what they want to achieve. Finally, traditional mainstream services provided by local agencies have been bypassed and remained largely unaffected by community safety initiatives.

205. The report has also attempted to paint a more positive picture of the many good practice achievements to date, and has drawn on these to tease out lessons – both at the local and national level – for addressing the current concerns.

206. Recommendations following from this analysis are set out at the end of this chapter. Although the report will be published at a time when local agencies are already developing their first three-year statutory strategies, it will be timely for partnerships to review their own performance after the first round of strategies for the Crime and Disorder Act, and to learn from others about the good practice available. The changes that are needed to make the most effective use of public money will take time to unfold, and so the recommendations have been divided into short- and medium-term actions. How and when partnerships choose to address these will depend to a large extent on the stage that they have reached: those just starting out on partnership working may take longer to reach the medium-term issues than those with plenty of experience already behind them.

207. Recommendations are also made at the national level. A realignment is needed at all levels of government to achieve a focus on the outcomes that matter to citizens. Once again, the need to support this major change is self-evident, and national departments that have configured around traditional service-based objectives must continue to develop their capacity to encourage and support local agencies in addressing issues that cut across traditional departmental boundaries.

208. In conclusion, local agencies have made a promising start in addressing the issue of community safety. However, any sustainable impact on the problem will take time to achieve and will require a long term commitment at all levels to working in partnership and investing in what works. New partnerships will not succeed overnight, and all involved will need to learn from their mistakes and overcome early problems inherent in such a major change in the way that public services work.

209. This report has been researched at a time of substantial changes both nationally and locally. The issue of 'what works' in promoting community safety was still largely unresolved at the time of this research. The absence of hard data both to define the problems and to catalogue 'what works' in addressing them has made it difficult to draw simple conclusions. What can be offered is an informed commentary and a way forward to improve understanding.

My poster is about things that I would like done to the Racecourse Estate

By Karl Oxberry, Gillas Lane Primary School

This picture was painted as part of a project carried out by Barnardos to find out what children on the Racecourse Estate in Sunderland liked, disliked and wished for in their community.

RECOMMENDATIONS

Promoting Community Safety

Recommendations for local partnerships

1   Engage with local communities

Short-term

- Take stock of existing consultation mechanisms.

- Identify target groups in high-crime areas that may require more support.

Medium-term

- Develop a two-way communications strategy.

- Include a media-management strategy.

- Develop more concerted approaches in high-crime areas.

2   Develop a culture of learning

Short-term

- Review whether audits have made best use of data across agencies, and have analysed hot spots and trends.

- Review literature, and what is known locally, on 'what works'.

Medium-term

- Develop a multi-agency information strategy for community safety.

- Develop a learning approach.

3   Develop an investment approach to community safety

Short-term

- Review and quantify major departmental activities on community safety.

- Review mechanisms to build community safety.

Medium-term

- Develop partnership joint investment plan.

- Develop capacity for cost-benefit analysis.

- Amend human resources policies to encorage the development of community safety.

RECOMMENDATIONS

Promoting Community Safety

4 **Develop accountable and delivery-focused partnerships**

Short-term

- Establish/review partnership constitution, vision and roles.

- Ensure clear reporting procedures for key projects.

- Review barriers to effective joint working, such as tenure of post.

Medium-term

- Review infrastructure for delivering strategic and operational priorities.

- Develop overall reporting mechanisms for partnership activities.

- Build reporting mechanisms into mainstream departmental work.

5 **Integrate community safety into the mainstream activities of public services**

Short-term

- Review individual departments' service objectives to ensure that they maximise their contribution to community safety.

- Identify lead agencies or departments to be accountable for elements of strategy.

Medium-term

- Encourage multi-agency working in high-crime areas.

- Encourage education, social services and health agencies to participate more fully.

- Look further afield to fire and transport as partners, as needed.

RECOMMENDATIONS

Promoting Community Safety

Recommendations for central government

1 **Support and encourage the development of learning about what works**

Short-term

- Continue to develop 'what works' databases.

- Encourage national training agencies to provide support to partnerships.

Medium-term

- Monitor performance nationally.

- Develop a dissemination strategy for 'what works'.

2 **Provide incentives to develop community safety work**

Short-term

- Ensure that any challenge funding encourages problem-solving and learning, rather than many one-off, unlinked initiatives.

Medium-term

- Develop range of incentives in national strategy.

- Continue to look for opportunities to divert money from justice to prevention and reducing offending.

3 **Ensure a corporate approach to community safety across central government**

Short-term

- Encourage a corporate view of community safety across Whitehall.

- Ensure that top-down strategies can be dovetailed with bottom-up approaches.

Medium-term

- Look for opportunities to encourage national strategies, only where a national approach can add value.

Appendix 1

Provisions for partnership working in the Crime and Disorder Act

Sections 5-7 and 17 of the Crime and Disorder Act

Crime and Disorder Strategies

5. (1) Subject to the provisions of this section, the functions conferred by section 6 below shall be exercisable in relation to each local government area by the responsible authorities, that is to say –

   a) the council for the area and, where the area is a district and the council is not a unitary authority, the council for the county which includes the district; and

   b) every chief officer of police any part of whose police area lies within the area.

   (2) In exercising those functions, the responsible authorities shall act in co-operation with the following persons and bodies, namely –

   a) every police authority any part of whose police area lies within the area;

   b) every probation committee or health authority any part of whose area lies within the area; and

   c) every person or body of a description which is for the time being prescribed by order of the Secretary of State under this subsection;

   and it shall be the duty of those persons and bodies to co-operate in the exercise by the responsible authorities of those functions.

   (3) The responsible authorities shall also invite the participation in their exercise of those functions of at least one person or body of each description which is for the time being prescribed by order of the Secretary of State under this subsection.

   (4) In this section and sections 6 and 7 below "local government area" means

   (a) in relation to England, each district or London borough, the City of London, the Isle of Wight and the Isles of Scilly;

   (b) in relation to Wales, each county or county borough.

6. (1) The responsible authorities for a local government area shall, in accordance with the provisions of section 5 above and this section, formulate and implement, for each relevant period, a strategy for the reduction of crime and disorder in the area.

   (2) Before formulating a strategy, the responsible authorities shall –

   (a) carry out a review of the levels and patterns of crime and disorder in the area (taking due account of the knowledge and experience of persons in the area);

(b) prepare an analysis of the results of that review;

(c) publish in the area a report of that analysis; and

(d) obtain the views on that report of persons or bodies in the area (including those of a description prescribed by order under section 5 (3) above), whether by holding public meetings or otherwise.

(3) In formulating a strategy, the responsible authorities shall have regard to the analysis prepared under subsection (2)(b) above and the views obtained under subsection (2) d) above.

(4) A strategy shall include –

a) objectives to be pursued by the responsible authorities, by co-operating persons or bodies or, under agreements with the responsible authorities, by other persons or bodies; and

b) long-term and short-term performance targets for measuring the extent to which such objectives are achieved.

(5) After formulating a strategy, the responsible authorities shall publish in the area a document which includes details of –

a) co-operating persons or bodies;

b) the review carried out under subsection (2) (a) above;

c) the report published under subsection (2)(c) above; and

d) the strategy, including in particular –

(i) the objectives mentioned in subsection (4)(a) above and, in each case, the authorities, persons or bodies by whom they are to be pursued; and

(ii) the performance targets mentioned in subsection (4)(b) above.

(6) While implementing a strategy, the responsible authorities shall keep it under review with a view to monitoring its effectiveness and making changes to it that appear necessary or expedient.

(7) In this section

"co-operating persons or bodies" means persons or bodies co-operating in the exercise of the responsible authorities' functions under this section;

"relevant period" means –

(a) the period of three years beginning with such day as the Secretary of State may by order appoint; and

(b) each subsequent period of three years.

7. (1) The responsible authorities for a local government area shall, whenever so required by the Secretary of State, submit to the Secretary of State a report on such matters connected with the exercise of their functions under section 6 above as may be specified in the requirement.

(2) A requirement under subsection (1) above may specify the form in which a report is to be given.

(3) The Secretary of State may arrange, or require the responsible authorities to arrange, for a report under subsection (1) above to be published in such manner as appears to him to be appropriate.

Miscellaneous and supplemental

17. (1) Without prejudice to any other obligation imposed on it, it shall be the duty of each authority to which this section applies to exercise its various functions with due regard to the likely effect of the exercise of those functions on, and the need to do all that it reasonably can to prevent, crime and disorder in its area.

(2) This section applies to a local authority, a joint authority, a police authority, a National Park authority and the Broards Authority.

(3) In this section –
"local authority" means a local authority within the meaning given by section 270(1) of the Local Government Act 1972 or the Common Council of the City of London;

"joint authority" has the same meaning as in the Local Government Act 1985;

"National Park authority" means an authority established under section 63 of the Environment Act 1995.

Appendix 2

Illustrative performance framework for 'Barset' crime and disorder partnership

	Area	Indicator
Overall outcomes	Quality of life	Public satisfaction with local area
	Fear of crime	Fear of crime survey
Underlying problems (examples)	Burglary	Burglaries per 1,000 population
	Racial harassment	Reporting levels, under-reporting
	Domestic violence	Reporting levels, under-reporting
	Graffiti and vandalism	Costs to public agencies
	Neighbour nuisance	Level of reporting to environmental health
	Youth disorder	Calls to police
Services	Police	Repeat victimisation Disorder incidents
	Social services	Protection for vulnerable people Youth justice preventive work
	Education	Truancy and exclusion levels
	Housing	Voids, turnover of tenancies
	Health	A&E admissions due to violence, drugs treatments
Partnership working	Budgets	Partnership investment plan
	Attendance	Key agency attendance
	Process	Constitution; lead agencies for key initiatives

Source: Audit Commission

Appendix 3

Advisory and technical groups

Advisory group

Dirk Aldous	Chief Constable, Dorset Constabulary (ACPO rep)
Mike Ashley	Local Government Association
Richard Arthur	Audit Commissioner
Julie Brett	Crime Prevention Agency, Home Office
Steve Brookes	HMIC
Mark Cadwallader	Welsh Local Government Association
Richard Childs	Crime Prevention Agency, Home Office (now Chief Constable, Lincolnshire Police)
Conal Devitt	Community Safety Co-ordinator, St Helens Borough Council
Sheila Douglas	Chief Executive, Taunton Dean Borough Council (SOLACE rep)
Fionnula Gill	Association of Police Authorities
Karin Phillips	SSP3, Welsh Office
Keith Povey	HMIC
Barry Webb	Police Research Group

Technical Group

John Burrows	Consultant, Morgan Harris Burrows
Martin Davies	London Borough of Merton (now with London Borough of Hackney)
Geoffrey Gibbs	Leicestershire Police
Andy Hayman	Essex Police (now with Metropolitan Police)
Mike Hough	Professor of Social Science, South Bank University
Gloria Laycock	Police Research Group
Martin Lewis	London Borough of Newham
Joyce Moseley	Consultant
Steve Osborne	Safe Neighbourhoods Unit
Sue Raikes	Thames Valley Partnership
Nick Tilley	Professor of Criminology, Nottingham Trent University

References

1. Audit Commission, *Misspent Youth: Young People and Crime*, Audit Commission, 1996.

2. Audit Commission, *Misspent Youth '98: The Challenge for Youth Justice*, Audit Commission, 1998.

3. Home Office, *Safer Communities: The Local Delivery of Crime Prevention Through the Partnership Approach*, London, Home Office, 1991 ('The Morgan report').

4. P Ekblom, 'The Conjunction of Criminal Opportunity – A Tool for Clear, Joined-up Thinking about Community Safety and Crime Reduction', in S Ballintyne et al (eds) *Key Issues in Crime Prevention, Crime Reduction and Community Safety*, IPPR, (forthcoming), summer 1999.

5. *Local Government Association Manifesto on Community Safety*, Local Government Association, 1997.

6. MORI, Analysis of 10 surveys of local concerns (unpublished), MORI, 1998.

7. Home Office, *The 1998 British Crime Survey, England and Wales*, *Home Office Statistical Bulletin*, Home Office Research, Development and Statistics Directorate, 1998.

8. US Department of Justice, *Crime and Justice in the United States and in England, 1981-1996*, Bureau of Justice Statistics, US Department of Justice, US, 1998.

9. T Hope, 'Community Safety, Crime and Disorder', in A Marlow and J Pitts (eds), *Planning Safer Communities*, Russell House Publishing, 1998, p174.

10. T Hope, 'Communities, Crime and Inequality in England and Wales', in T Bennett (ed), *Preventing Crime and Disorder*, Institute of Criminology, Cambridge Cropwood Series, University of Cambridge, 1996.

11. G Farrell, K Pease, Police Research Group, *Once Bitten, Twice Bitten: Repeat Victimisation and Its Implications for Crime Prevention*, Police Research Group Paper No. 26, Home Office, 1993.

12. Home Office, *British Crime Survey*, Home Office, 1988.

13. Home Office, Research Findings No. 93, *Concern About Crime: Findings from the 1998 British Crime Survey*, Home Office Research, Development and Statistics Directorate, 1998.

14. By kind permission of the Henley Centre for Forecasting, *Planning for Social Change 1998: Understanding Trends and Influences Affecting The Consumer Environment*, 1998.

15. Department of Environment, Transport and the Regions (DETR), *A New Deal for Transport: Better for Everyone* (The Government's White Paper on the Future of Transport), DETR, July 1998.

16. Social Exclusion Unit, *Bringing Britain Together: A National Strategy for Neighbourhood Renewal*, The Stationery Office, September 1998.

17. A Leigh, T Read, N Tilley, *Problem-oriented Policing: Brit Pop*, Home Office Police Research Group Paper No. 75, 1996.

18. Home Office, HMIC statistics on 'standard incidents', 1995/96-1997/98 (unpublished).

19. Chartered Institute of Environmental Health Officers, 'Noise Monitoring and Control Figures 1992/93 – 1996/97', from annual reports on the work of local authority environmental health departments in England and Wales 1988 (unpublished).

20. Social Landlords Crime and Nuisance Group, *Antisocial Behaviour in England, 1996-1997: A Report on Patterns and Problems in Tackling Anti-Social Neighbours*, 1998 (unpublished).

21. J Q Wilson and G Kelling, 'Broken Windows', *Atlantic Monthly*, March 1982, pp29-38.

22. W Skogan, *Disorder and Decline: Crime and the Spiral of Decay in American Neighbourhoods*, University of California Press, USA, 1990.

23. HM Treasury, *Comprehensive Spending Review*, Chapter 10, July 1998.

24. International Centre for the Prevention of Crime (ICPC), *Police and Prevention: Towards Common Grounds*, Background paper prepared for first seminar, ICPC conference, Montreal, November 1998, p11.

25. Association of British Insurers, *General Business Statistics: Claims Results Quarter 1 1998*, Association of British Insurers, May 1998.

26. British Retail Consortium, *Retail Crime Costs Survey 1995/1996*, British Retail Consortium, 1997.

27. Economist, 'Welcome to the New World of Private Security', *The Economist Newspaper Ltd*, 19 April 1997.

28. Accounts Commission for Scotland, *A Safer Place: Property Risk Management in Schools*, Accounts Commission for Scotland, January 1997.

29. E Stanko, D Crisp, C Hale and H Lucraft, Counting the Costs: *Estimating the Impact of Domestic Violence in the London Borough of Hackney*, Crime Concern, 1998.

30. N Davidson, 'Costing Crime and Crime Prevention', paper presented to the British Criminology Conference, Loughborough, July 1995 (unpublished).

31. NHS Executive, *A Common Framework to Identify the Costs of Crime in NHS Trusts*, Guidance Note, NHS Executive, July 1997.

32. Health Services Advisory Committee, *Violence and Aggression to Staff in the Health Services*, Department of Health, December 1997; and NHS Executive Guidance, *Effective Management of Security in A&E Departments*, NHS Executive, May 1997.

33. Home Office, Department of Education and Science, Department of Environment, Department of Health and Social Security and Welsh Office, *Crime Prevention* (Home Office Circular 8/1984), Home Office, 1984.

34. Home Office, *Crime and Disorder Act 1998*, Home Office, July 1998.

35. J Bright, *Turning the Tide: Crime, Community and Crime Prevention*, Demos, 1997, p12 and p39.

36. Audit Commission, *Helping With Enquiries: Tackling Crime Effectively*, London, HMSO, 1993, p14.

37. Her Majesty's Inspectorate of Constabulary, *Beating Crime: HMIC Thematic Review of Crime Prevention*, Home Office, March 1998.

38. Local Government Management Board, *Survey of Community Safety Activities in Local Government in England and Wales*, LGMB, July 1996.

39. A Hirschfield and K Bowers, University of Liverpool, and K Pease, University of Huddersfield, Community Safety Survey of 36 police forces and 223 local authorities in England and Wales, March 1998 (unpublished).

40. Home Office, *News Release 282/98: £250 million to Develop an Effective Crime Reduction Strategy of the Future*, Home Office, July 1998.

41. S Chenery, J Holt, K Pease, *Biting Back II: Reducing Repeat Victimisation in Huddersfield*, Crime Detection and Prevention Series Paper No. 82, Home Office Police Research Group, 1997.

42. A M Liddle, L R Gelsthorpe, *Inter-agency Crime Prevention: Further Issues*, PRG Supplementary Paper to CPU Series Papers Nos. 52 and 53, Home Office Crime Prevention Unit, 1994.

43. A Sampson and C Phillips, *Preventing Repeat Racial Victimisation on an East London Estate*, Police Research Group Paper No. 67, Home Office, July 1995.

44. L Sherman et al, *Preventing Crime: What Works, What Doesn't, What's Promising*, US Dept of Justice, Office of Justice Programs, US, February 1997.

45. P Ekblom and K Pease, 'Evaluating Crime Prevention', in M Tonry and D P Farrington (eds), *'Building a Safer Society', Crime and Justice*, Vol. 19, University of Chicago Press, 1995, pp585-6.

46. P 6, 'Problem-solving Government', in I Hargreaves and I Christie (eds), *Tomorrow's Politics: The Third Way and Beyond*, Demos, 1998, pp56-58.

47. CIPFA, *Local Government Statistics* and *Police Statistics*, Actuals, 1996-97, CIPFA, 1997.

48. Audit Commission, *A Fruitful Partnership: Effective Partnership Working*, Audit Commission, 1998.

49. S Loftus, PhD on Community Safety (unpublished), 1997.

50. Home Office Community Fire Safety Task Force, *Safe as Houses, The Report of the Community Fire Safety Task Force*, Home Office, 1997, p10.

51. A M Liddle, L R Gelsthorpe, *Crime Prevention and Inter-agency Co-operation*, PRG CPU Series Paper No. 53, Home Office Crime Prevention Unit, 1994, pp8-9.

52. Home Office, *Digest 3: Information on the Criminal Justice System in England and Wales*, Home Office, 1995.

53. UK Anti-drugs Co-ordination Unit, White Paper, *Tackling Drugs to Build a Better Britain: The Government's 10-year Strategy for Tackling Drug Abuse*, The Stationery Office, April 1998.

54. See, for example, M Hough and N Tilley, *Getting the Grease to Squeak: Research Lessons for Prevention*, Home Office Police Research Group Paper No. 85, Home Office, 1998, pp2-6.

55. A Power and R Tunstall, *Swimming Against the Tide: Polarisation or Progress on 20 Unpopular Council Estates 1980-1995*, Joseph Rowntree Foundation, 1995.

56. L E Cohen and M Felson, 'Social Change and Crime Rate Trends: A Routine Activities Approach' in *American Sociological Review* 44, 1998 pp588-608. See also Ref. 4 above for a more sophisticated model.

57. Home Office, *Guidance on Statutory Crime and Disorder Partnerships: Crime and Disorder Act 1998*, Home Office, July 1998.

58. See, for example, D Forrester, M Chatterton, K Pease, R Brown, *The Kirkholt Burglary Project, Rochdale*, Home Office Crime Prevention Unit Paper No. 13, London, Home Office, 1988.

59. Home Office, *Reducing Offending: An Assessment of Research Evidence on Ways of Dealing with Offending Behaviour*, Home Office Research Study No. 187, Home Office, 1998.

60. Home Office, *Safer Cities and Domestic Burglary*, Home Office Research Study No. 164, Home Office, 1996.

Index References are to paragraph numbers, Boxes, Case Studies and Appendices

W

Y

Z